24 Router Projects

2nd Edition

24 Router Projects

2nd Edition

Percy W. Blandford

TAB Books
Division of McGraw-Hill, Inc.
Blue Ridge Summit, PA 17294-0850

SECOND EDITION
FIRST PRINTING

Library of Congress Cataloging-in-Publication Data

Blandford, Percy W.
    24 router projects / by Percy W. Blandford.—2nd ed.
      p. cm.
    Includes index.
    ISBN 0-8306-4546-2
    1. Routers (Tools) 2. Woodwork. I. Title. II. Title: Twenty-
four router projects.
TT203.5.B55 1993
684.1'042—dc20   93-27576
                                          CIP

Acquisitions editor: April Nolan
Editorial team: Joanne Slike, Executive Editor
                Lori Flaherty, Managing Editor
                Robert Burdette, Editor
Production team: Katherine G. Brown, Director
                  Tina M. Sourbier, Typesetting
                  Rose McFarland, Layout
                  Joann Woy, Indexer
Design team: Jaclyn J. Boone, Designer
              Brian Allison, Associate Designer
Cover design: Sandra Blair Design, Harrisburg, Pa.
Cover photo: Brent Blair, Harrisburg, Pa.

                                                  HT1
                                                  4488

Contents

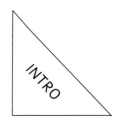

THE HAND ROUTER, a simple type of plane for leveling the bottoms of grooves and recesses, has been around for a long time. Its wooden version, known as an "old woman's tooth" because of its single projecting blade, was an essential tool in the kit of a medieval cabinetmaker. Electric routers with built-in motors followed; they could do similar work as well as a few other operations. They were valuable portable power tools, but in recent years there have been many developments in routers and the bits or cutters for them.

Routers are available in several sizes and powers, with collet capacity a guide to size. Although a lighter tool is easier to handle for work within its capacity, powerful routers are needed for some of the more advanced bits now available. *Plunging* is useful for making cuts in stages. Adaptors may fit smaller bits into large collets, but it is important for safety and wear on the equipment not to attempt larger or heavier cuts than the router's design allows.

Many of the advances in the versatility of the router in recent years are due to the development of carbide-tipped bits, which are able to stand up to heavy use without blunting. Plain tool steels do not remain sharp very long on some abrasive woods or man-made materials such as particleboard where the bonding resin will soon wear a cutting edge. Carbide tips stand up to this work for a long time, even longer on milder woods.

The projects in this book take advantage of the great variety of router bits now available. With some bits you can cut dadoes of many sizes and forms, including dovetail sections, many molding sections, and rabbets or grooves for panels. There are reverse-pattern cutters that cut the end of one part of a frame to fit another. There are bits to cut internal and external profiles and trim or chamfer edges. Many joints may be cut with a router—in addition to the traditional ones, some that take advantage of the facilities of a router.

Raised panels in doors are attractive but difficult to make with the usual tools in a small workshop. Panel-raising router bits will do the work accurately, but it is important to follow the maker's instructions for safety and efficiency.

All the projects in this book have been designed so that most of the constructional and decorative work can be done with router cutters. In some cases there are alternative methods if you do not have every bit needed or suitable guides for a particular operation. Because many of the projects can be made with comparatively small pieces of wood, they are inexpensive. If a beginner's early attempts are not as successful as he or she would wish, the loss of money is not great. Some projects call for more advanced skills, but all are possible for a moderately competent user with a variety of bits.

The second edition of this book has been updated to take into account recent router developments. There are five new projects incorporating a considerable amount of router work. This is a project book, complete in itself, but it is not an instruction manual on the router. Anyone wishing to learn about router techniques should read *The Portable Router Book;* 2nd edition (TAB 4432), by R. J. DeCristoforo.

Safety

- Make sure that the workpiece is firmly held and that you can maintain your balance throughout the cutting operation.

- Concentrate on what you are doing, and do not be distracted by other matters.

- Check the condition of your router, its lead and plug. Keep it dry and never work in wet conditions. Remove the plug when changing cutters.

- Make sure the router bit is secure in its collet and that any keys or wrenches have been removed.

- Wear eye protection. With dusty materials or prolonged work sessions, wear a breathing mask. Ear protection is also advisable.

- Keep children away while you are using the router.

- Observe the maker's maintenance instructions and store the router where it cannot be damaged by other tools.

Stands and pads

PLANTS STAND on a windowsill, coffee or teapots in the kitchen, or hot pads for the table can be made from small pieces of solid wood, plywood, or veneered particleboard. With these projects, you can use offcuts too small for other purposes. First-time router users can experiment because mistakes are not costly.

Particleboard with wood or plastic veneer on one or both sides can be edged with wood and used either side up. If you are planning to make several pads, it is easier to prepare the edges of large or long pieces, before cutting to size. The tongued wood is easier to hold if you work on the edge of a wide board, then saw after cutting the tongue. Pads can be any size or shape.

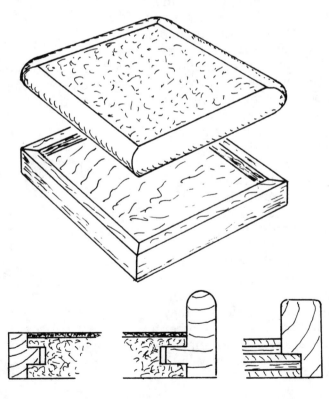

Groove the particleboard slightly deeper than the tongue so the surfaces can close tightly. Outer edges can be left square or rounded. Miter the corners and glue the assembly.

A stand for a tea- or coffeepot might be better with a raised rim. You could extend a tongued rim upward or work rabbets for the joints. One way of providing a heat-resistant base is to mount a ceramic tile on plywood and frame.

A block of wood with grooves across makes a functional and decorative stand. You can cut grooves with V, round, or flat bottoms and arrange just a few one way or cross them more closely to make a pattern of squares or diamonds.

If the wood is thick, you can make patterns on both sides. Edges and corners can be square or rounded. If there is much grooving, molded edges directly over them are inappropriate. Most hardwoods should be strong enough when grooved closely, but if you are using softwood, keep the grooves shallow and wide apart.

If you want a molded edge, cut rabbets all round and work a molding on the rabbeted parts. You can also use two thicknesses of wood, because it is easier to work the molded edges on a separate piece.

For an interesting effect that provides insulation and ventilation for a hot pad, work grooves from both sides so they cross and break into each other to produce spaces. The example shows three stopped grooves each way, but you can use any number. With a larger number, much of the wood would be covered with pierced holes within the grooves.

Cut the grooves on each side so that they are slightly deeper than half the thickness of the wood. If you cut them so that opposite grooves just meet, you might have to clean out raggedness in the holes. If you cut too deep, the effect is not as attractive. This pad can be used either way up, so if you do any edge decoration, it should be symmetrical.

Stands or pads don't have to be square. A round outline can be attractive because most items set on it are likely to be round. If you can turn the disk on a lathe or have a radius device for your router, consider a round outline. Cutting a circle freehand, will make any discrepancies of the outline apparent. A hexagon or octagon would be a good choice for a stand. Use a rectangle with its corners cut off for long dishes.

If the pad or stand is to go under a vase or pot that might leak water, you can provide a groove near the edges to catch water before it runs onto the table.

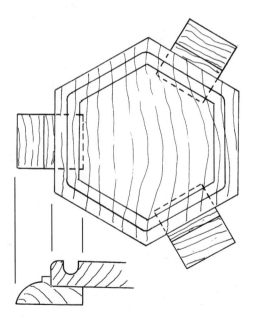

A hexagonal stand with a grooved border or other routed decoration could be used without further embellishment, but you might want to provide feet, molded however you wish. The feet can be glued underneath or located with rabbets.

Three feet will stand without wobbling on any surface. Most surfaces are flat, but if there is unevenness, four feet would wobble.

Screwing tackle box

THE ABILITY of straight router cutters to form clean, accurate grooves can be used to make storage places for many small tools, particularly those that should be kept apart so they do not become blunted by rubbing together. This applies to drills, many small metalworking and model-making tools, and sets of taps and dies where a compartmented box not only protects the tools but prevents them from being lost.

The example shown holds five sizes of dies and their stock with accompanying taps and wrench. You can assemble your tools and plan a box to suit. The arrangement shown will serve as a guide to procedure. Lay out the tools and try different ways of arranging them to get the size. Do not make slots too close, or the wood between may be weakened.

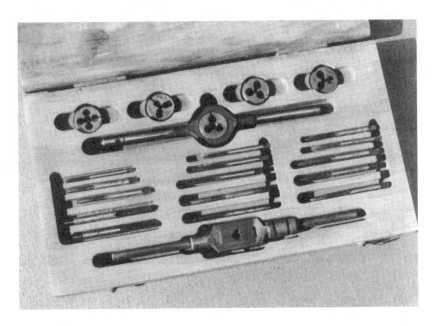

Choose a close-grained wood without flaws. A coarse-grained or soft wood may break out or leave rough edges. Allow sufficient thickness for there to be about ¼ inch under the deepest slot. In the example, the slots are cut in wood ¾-inch thick and 6 inches by 11 inches. All the tools fit into this thickness, and the lid is a piece about ½ inch thick. If tools have thick parts, as they will if you are making a box for router cutters, you may have to allow for matching hollows in the lid, so it would have to be thicker.

- Cut the wood to size with carefully squared ends. Cut the lid to the same size. Both parts can have rounded corners.

- Mark the centerlines of the grooves and their limits and hole centers where appropriate.

- Drill for the dies and the die stock. Allow about ⅟₁₆-inch clearance in diameter and depth. If you do not have a suitable router bit, these hollows are best drilled with a *Forstner bit*, which does not leave the deep center depression of other bits.

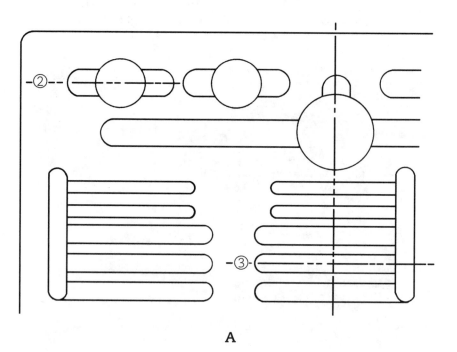

A

- The finger hollows on each side of a die can be the same width as that for the arms of the die stock. Make these hollows deep enough for finger and thumb to grip the dies. The die-stock arms should sink below the surface but allow a small finger slot for lifting the center of the stock.

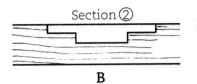

Section ②

B

- The tap-wrench recess may be treated in a similar way to the die stock, the ends deep enough to take the arms and a deeper center portion.

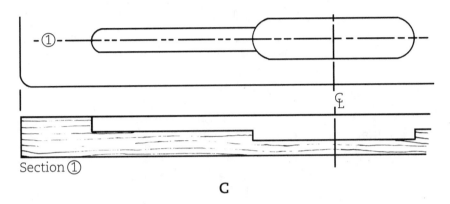

Section ①

C

- The slots for the taps can vary in width and length if necessary. Each tap projects into a crosswise slot and is released by pressing down that end, so the crosswise slots should be deeper. Make the crosswise slots first, using the router guide against the end of the wood. Cut the tap grooves into these grooves.

Section ③

D

- Check that the tools fit and can be removed easily. Sand the wood for both parts.

- Hinge the lid to the box. Two 1½-inch hinges on the rear edges should be satisfactory, but you can let them in if you wish. Two hook fasteners at the front will keep the box closed.

Materials List

1 box	¾ × 6 × 11
1 lid	½ × 6 × 11

CHAPTER 3

Router lettering

A ROUTER CUTTER can be used instead of a chisel and gouges to make carved lettering. Letters formed by grooves in wood will catch the light so that shadows emphasize the shapes. Traditional hand-carved lettering is formed of **V** grooves, but a similar effect can be obtained with grooves of other cross sections. You can experiment with cutters you have, but do not choose any that round the edges because it is the shadows cast by hard edges that give prominence to the letters.

A flat-bottomed groove may be used, but a rounded one looks better. A **V** section is nearer to the shape obtained by hand carving. The rounded section is commonest and very effective if it is cut at least as deep as it is wide.

A

You may exercise your artistic expression by laying out freehand lettering, but this must be well done if it is to be effective. Sometimes you will be aiming at a casual effect, as when providing directions on a trail among trees. For more formal lettering, if you do not trust your artistic ability, it is better to rely on a geometric layout.

B

There are books of lettering for hand carvers that you can use as guides, but many of these letters have *serifs*, angular projections at the corners, and cannot be cut with a router. If you want to include serifs, you must follow the router cuts with a chisel.

It is possible to get guides for lettering with routers. The simplest is like a stencil. A more elaborate type has the router mounted in a machine; you follow the pattern with a point, and the router repeats it in the wood. If you intend to go into production with many signs, one of these pattern machines is advisable, but if you are considering doing router lettering only occasionally, the technique must be simpler.

A satisfactory form of lettering without flourishes or unusual shapes can be laid out using a pattern of squares in which the letters are three units wide and five units high, the unit being the width of the router cutter. Nearly all letters fit into this proportion. The letter *I* is obviously narrower, and you may wish to make *M* and *W* slightly wider. Numbers will also suit these proportions. If you use a ½-inch cutter, most letters will be 1½ inches wide by 2½ inches high. If you allow ½ inch between letters, you can calculate the space a word will need and adjust the total layout accordingly.

Draw a pattern of lines forming five lines of squares. Many angular letters such as *E* and *H* can be drawn in immediately, then the router will follow to make the letters with rounded ends.

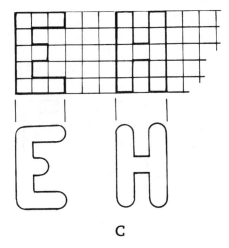

C

Letters like O, S, and B, which include curves, require marked centers. Then draw the shapes with compasses, and your cutter follows these lines. (See illustration D below.)

Sloping lines are simple, but avoid leaving very small pieces or narrow angles by keeping the bar of A low and making M and W wider. (See illustration E below.)

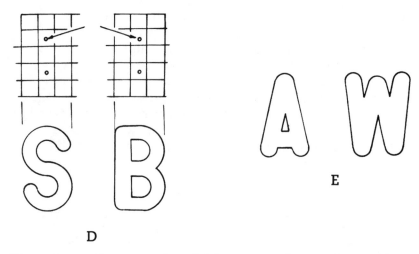

D

E

The patterns shown produce fairly compact letters that can be cut satisfactorily in close-grained hardwood. If you want larger letters of lesser width, you can use a similar layout to get the letter shapes, but cut with a narrower cutter. This more open pattern reduces the risk of breaking out coarse grain and produces lettering more easily read at a distance.

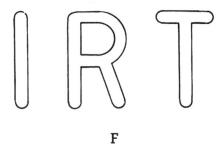

F

When cutting lettering laid out in this way, you can work entirely freehand, but to get truly accurate straight lines, clamp a straightedge on the wood as a guide where the edge cannot be used. It is advisable to cut all tops and bottoms of letters using a guide so that a complete word is straight. Slight inaccuracies in other directions will not be as noticeable.

Router lettering can be cut in a plain rectangular piece of wood, and that may be all that is required, but with a router you can choose various outlines and decorate the edges in many ways. There may be a special shape applicable to the name, but in most cases the outline should be symmetrical. The important feature is the lettering so be careful not to detract attention by overelaborating the outline and decoration of the wood.

With square corners, there is a risk of damage, so they may be cut off. (See A below) You can round them. This is appropriate if there are corner fixing screws. (See B below.) An alternative is to hollow the corners. (See C below.) The edges need not be straight, but do not curve very deeply. (See D below.)

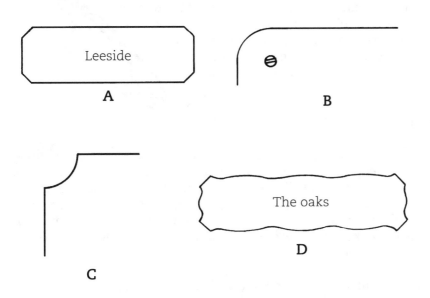

Besides cutting the letters, you can work a border with the router. Keep it narrow and parallel to the edge, whether this is straight or shaped. Corner screws can become part of the decoration.

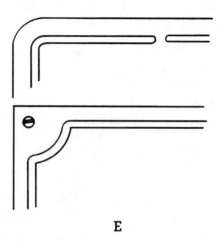

E

Some signs are made from pieces cut across a log. This can be very effective, particularly if the cut is made at an acute angle so that the face to be lettered is elliptical. Unfortunately, many woods cut in this way develop cracks as they dry. Do not be tempted to start work on recently cut wood. Leave it to dry for several months. It's advisable to have several pieces drying in case some have to be discarded.

F

A sign made from a flat board can have square edges, but with a router you can decorate by *molding*. The molding you use depends on the available cutters, but almost any molding is possible. If the wood is large in relation to the lettering, you can make the molding wide. Otherwise, it is better kept compact. In general, keep the back of the board full-size and let the molding slope to the front.

When all lettering and molding has been done, the front surface should be skimmed with a sharp plane, then sanded. Check that all hollows are smooth.

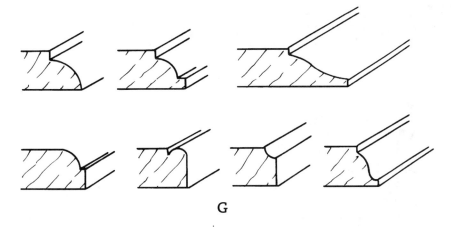

G

The wood can be left untreated for some situations, but usually it is better protected. Varnish will protect without affecting the sharpness of the letters. Paint tends to lessen the effect of the letters. Light and shade may be all that is needed to make the lettering prominent. Contrast can be increased by painting inside the letter grooves. If this is a dark color and the surface is finished with clear varnish, the effect can be attractive and draw attention to the wording. Use a thick paint in the grooves; thin paint may soak into the end grain and spoil the surface appearance.

Incised lettering of this type is probably best done in a quality solid wood, but there are alternatives. Thick plywood might be used with paint in the grooves and a frame around the outer edges. For a modern effect, plywood may be surfaced with Formica or another plastic, the letters cut through into the wood. Paint the grooves in a contrasting color.

Letters can also be cut into Plexiglas, clear or colored. The matte lettering will contrast with the bright surface. Backlighting may be used with clear or translucent Plexiglas. This material requires perfect work, or flaws will be obvious. Cuts need not be very deep, but it is advisable to use a guide for the router. More ideas for router lettering are shown in chapter 20.

CHAPTER 4

Colonial shelves

A STRAIGHT ROUTER cutter works dadoes, and the obvious use of dadoes is to fit shelves. There are many types of shelving projects, but this example follows a commonly used design of colonial and early American days. The pioneer woodworker had to cut his joints and add decoration with hand tools. A router speeds the work and ensures accuracy, making possible edge decoration that would be tedious to do by hand.

Solid wood is used throughout, and all parts may be ⅝ inch thick for the overall sizes suggested. Books are heavy and will make thin shelves sag in time, so use sound wood of adequate thickness. The back is open to the wall. If you want to close it, cut rabbets in the sides for hardboard or thin plywood. The piece above the top shelf stiffens the assembly and can be used for screws into the wall.

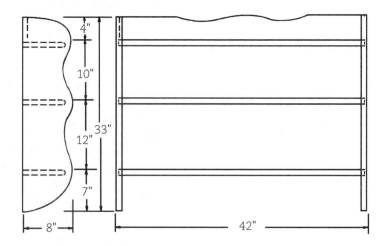

- The sides are the key parts. Mark them out , but do not cut the shaped edges yet. (Shown right.)

- Make the three shelves 7 inches wide, with lengths to go halfway into the sides.

- Cut dadoes for the shelves in the sides to half thickness.

- Round the front edges of the shelves to match the ends of the dadoes. Drill each shelf end for two screws upward through the dadoes to reinforce the glued joints when you assemble.

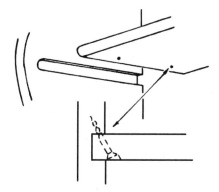

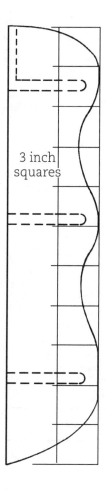

3 inch squares

- Make the top piece the same length as the shelves. It fits above the top shelf and requires a rabbet in each side. The wood may be left parallel or have its top edge shaped. (Shown at the top of the next page.)

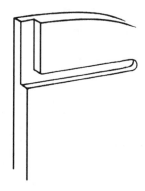

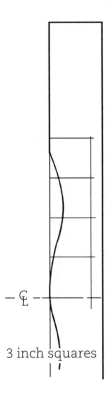

3 inch squares

- Cut the front edges of the sides to shape. They may be rounded in cross section or decorated with any other pattern for which you have a router cutter. The shaped edge of the top part may be rounded, but for certain designs a molding is appropriate. (Shown at left.)

- Another way to strengthen the joints if you have suitable cutters is with *dovetail dadoes*, which have ample strength without screws.

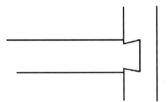

- It might be sufficient to glue the top piece to the rear edge of the top shelf, or you may drill upward for two or three screws.

- Assemble all parts with glue and screws. Check squareness by measuring diagonals and sight across to see that there is no twist.

- Drill the top piece for hanging screws. Finish with polish or paint to suit the wood or surroundings.

2 sides	⅝ × 8 × 34	
3 shelves	⅝ × 7 × 42	**Materials list**
1 top	⅝ × 4 × 42	

Cutlery box

A BOX FOR carrying knives and forks or other utensils is useful to take barbecue items into the yard or carry tools. This box is a convenient size for anything up to carving knives, but its measurements can be adapted to suit your largest items.

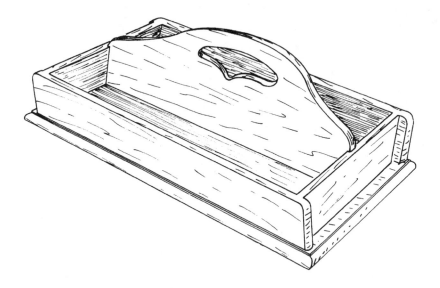

Use a good-quality hardwood, which can be given a clear finish for an attractive box that can be displayed in the kitchen or dining room. This could be ½ inch thick for all parts, but if you choose softwood, it would be better to increase the thickness.

The router can be used for profiling, joints, and molding edges. When marking out, allow the dado joints to be half the thickness of the wood. The ends fit into the sides ½ inch back from their ends.

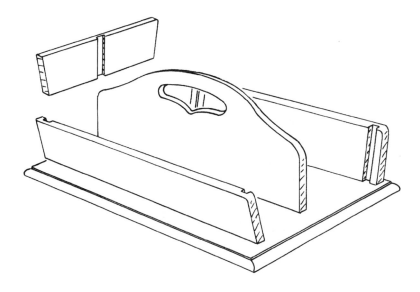

- Mark out the main sizes of the center division. This controls the size of some other parts (see below).

- Mark out the pair of ends. The angle of each end is ½ inch in the 3-inch width. Mark the central dadoes that will take the division (see the top of next page).

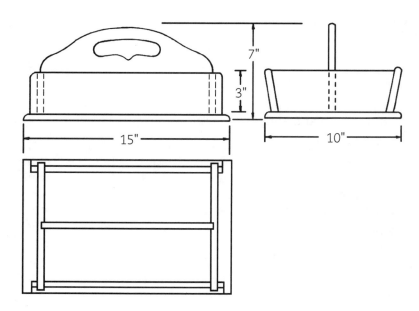

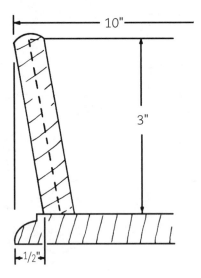

- From the slope of an end obtain the width of wood needed for the sides. Plane the lower edges to fit against the bottom. Cut a moderate curve along the top edges. Cut a matching curve across the top edges of the ends.

- Cut all dadoes. Round the top corners of the sides and continue the curved edge over the ends.

- Shape the outside of the center division.

- Make the hand hole with a *plunge router cutter*. The amount of curve to allow at the bottom may have to be adjusted to suit the diameter of the cutter.

- Round the outer and inner edges with the same curve used on the sides and ends for a comfortable grip.

- Assemble all parts made so far. If you have cut tight joints, glue alone will provide adequate strength. When the bottom is screwed on, it will reinforce the carcass joints. If you want to add strength to joints, drive pins from outside, set them below the surface, and cover them with wood filler. Check squareness and see that bottom edges are level.

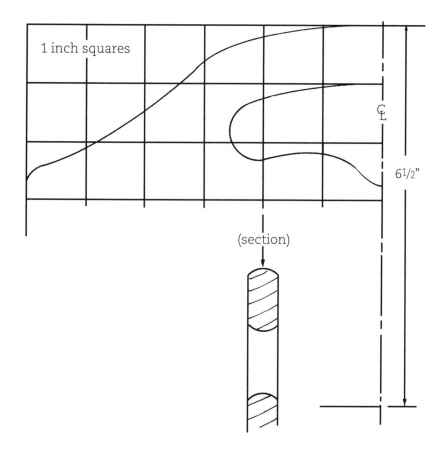

1 inch squares

(section)

₵̶L̶

6¹/₂"

- Make the bottom to project ½ inch all around. Its edges may be rounded in the same way as other exposed edges, or you can use a simple molding. An elaborate molding would be inappropriate.

- Attach the bottom with glue and screws. For cutlery, you might wish to stain and varnish or polish the wood before attaching the bottom, then glue cloth to the top surface of the bottom to provide a lining inside. Trim off any that extends after screwing on.

1 division	½ × 6½ × 14
2 ends	½ × 3 × 10
2 sides	½ × 3½ × 15
1 bottom	½ × 10 × 16

Materials list

CHAPTER 6

Coffee table

A SMALL TABLE provides plenty of scope for the use of a router, in both construction and decoration. This coffee table has its legs chamfered. The edges of the top are cut in a wavy pattern and molded. Its surface is also decorated with an incised pattern. The rails are shown with edges shaped to match the top. Construction should be with hardwood. To allow for possible expansion and contraction of the top, the table is held by buttons that can slide in grooves in the top rails.

Sizes are suggested, but you might want to modify them to suit your materials or needs. The same methods of construction and decoration can be used for tables of very different sizes. You may vary some decorations or omit some. You can turn the legs instead of chamfering them. These instructions are for a coffee table of the size and pattern as drawn.

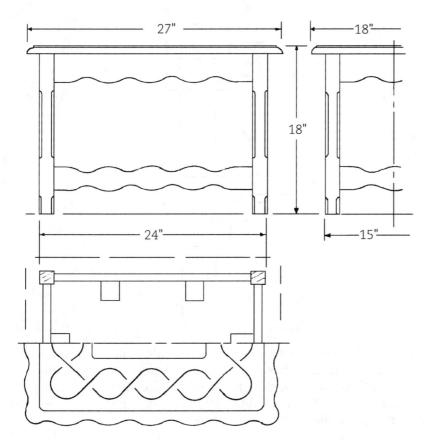

- Mark out a set of legs with the positions of rails and the limits of chamfers, but do not mark joint details until the rails are ready to be marked as well. Leave a little extra wood at the tops of the legs until after the framework has been assembled.

- Prepare the wood for the rails, but do not decorate the edges until the joints have been cut. Joints to the legs can be done with mortises and tenons or dowels. Mark and cut or drill the rails to match each other. Barefaced tenons should be strong enough to meet in the legs, but dowels should be taken far enough to miter against each other. (See the top of next page.)

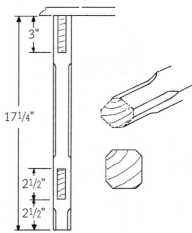

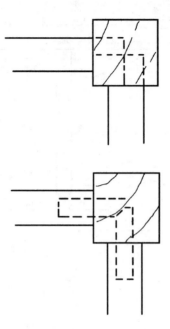

- Groove the inner surfaces of the top rails to take the buttons. You will probably find it is simplest to groove the full length of the rails, but you can groove just in the intended vicinity of the buttons. If you do, allow some excess length in the grooves so the buttons can move.

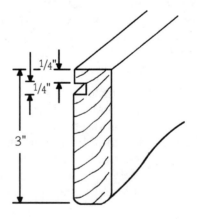

1/4"

1/4"

3"

- You will probably have to glue boards to make up the width of the top. Edge and surface outlines are shown. Draw this quarter-size pattern to a size to suit your wood. Draw centerlines both ways on the surface of the wood and transfer the design. The rails will have the same edge shaping.

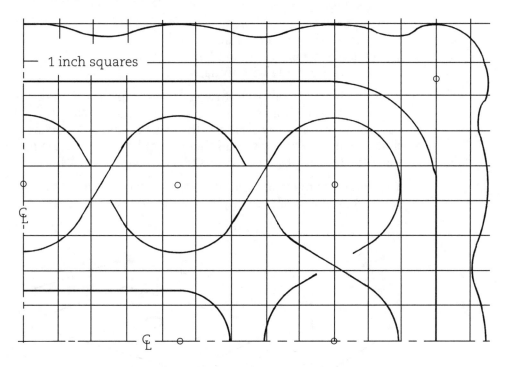

1 inch squares

- To ensure a regular matching pattern throughout all parts, make a template of an edge to extend over at least three curves and use that to mark or check all shaped edges.

- Sand all parts of the framing and assemble them. To get squareness all around, first assemble the two opposite long sides squarely to match each other. When the glue has set, add the rails the other way and square the assembly end and top.

- Mold the edges of the top. This can be any pattern you wish, but do not make it very wide. Cut the design on the top with **V** grooves 60 degrees or 90 degrees and not very deep. Appearance may depend on the choice of wood, but a depth of ⅛ inch should be enough. Experiment on scrapwood. The central area of the top is shown plain, but you can incise a badge or emblem there or personalize the table with initials.

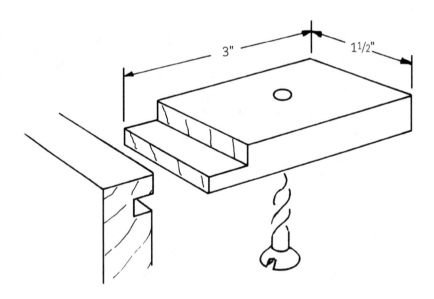

- It should be sufficient to put two buttons into each long rail and one in each short rail, but you can use more. Make the buttons with tongues to slide in the grooves and a thickness that will allow a screw to pull the top tight to the rails. Do not force the buttons to the bottoms of the rail grooves.

- You will probably want to make a trial assembly, but it will be easier to apply finish to the parts if you remove the top.

4 legs	1½ × 1½ × 18
2 rails	¾ × 3 × 24
2 rails	¾ × 3 × 15
2 rails	¾ × 2½ × 24
2 rails	¾ × 2½ × 15
buttons	½ × 1½ × 20

Oilstone cases

To GET THE BEST EDGE on woodworking cutting tools,
you need three stones used with oil or water. A coarse stone
quickly revives a dull edge or cuts back a notch caused by
hitting a nail. The medium stone produces an edge that may be
good enough for some purposes, but for the sharpest cuts and
best wood surface, the fine stone should follow.

Stones used for plane irons and chisels measure about $1 \times 2 \times 8$
inches and are best mounted in wood cases with lids. A case
may be a built-up box, but traditionally it is cut from solid
wood. Before the introduction of portable routers, this box had
to be made fairly laboriously and not always very accurately
with several hand tools. A router will cut the hollows for the
stone in box and lid easily and accurately and can be used to
decorate the lid and do other work.

If you only have one stone, its box can have a simple section.
The box recess should fit the stone close enough to prevent it
moving about, but it is useful to be able to lift the stone to turn
it over or use its edge. The lid should be an easy fit on the
stone. The sides need not be very wide, but the ends may
extend for strength and to allow a tool that is inadvertently
taken over the end of the stone to drop on wood so that its edge
will not be damaged.

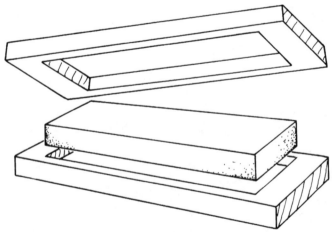

You can make three independent cases, but with a router it is easy to make them link together.

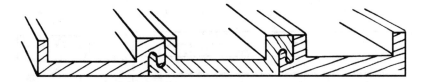

If you fit them between stop pieces on the bench, you have a battery of stones ready for use, but yet you can remove any stone in its case when it is needed elsewhere.

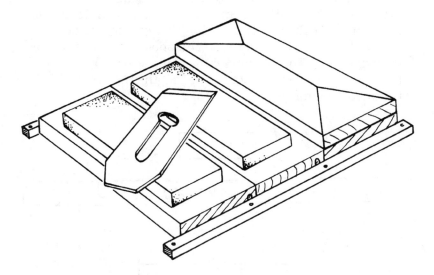

Any wood can be used, but an attractive hardwood is easier to work accurately than softwood and looks good if varnished for appearance and to prevent the absorption of oil or water.

You can make any number of linked cases; the instructions for three may easily be adapted to other numbers. It is assumed that the stones are 2 × 8 inches.

- Prepare the wood for the cases.

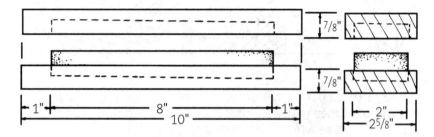

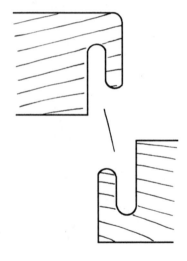

The extra width to allow for the joints depends on your available cutters. The two linking hooked parts need not total more than ¾ inch, (shown left), but that can be altered. Allow for two links on the center case and one on each outside case (shown below). The lids are all the same size (shown at bottom of page). Allow some extra length on all parts, to be trimmed off later.

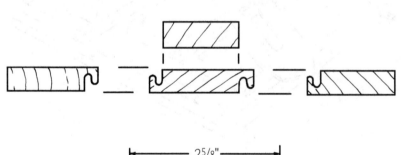

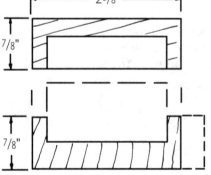

- Mark out the recesses for the stones, a little less than half its depth in the case. You will probably prefer to remove most of the waste freehand, then trim the edges of the recesses with the aid of guides. Adjust sizes so the stones can be lifted out of the cases and make the lids a loose fit.

- Cut the edge joints. If you do not have a router cutter to make complete hooks in one pass, the grooves may be cut, then the hooks reduced to size and rounded. Aim to make a fairly loose fit. It should not be necessary to press the parts together.

- Cut the wood to length to complete the cases.

- The recessed lids may be finished in several ways. They are adequately functional if left with square edges, but they provide an opportunity for using decorative cutters.

- Slopes to a central ridge may be planed or cut with a tool intended for raised panels. A narrower raised band can leave a flat top. A small rounding can have a shallow groove inside it. (Shown bottom left.)

- Any small molding can be cut around the top edges. You can cut a small bead around the lower edges. A hollow around the sides will provide a grip for lifting the lid. (Shown bottom right.)

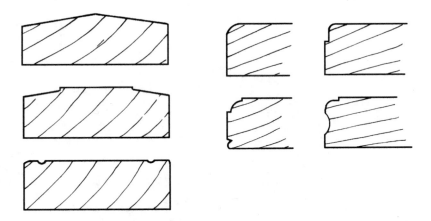

- When the stones are used between the guide strips, they are unlikely to move.

- If you want to use a stone elsewhere, a strip of leather or rubber glued under each end will reduce the risk of slipping.

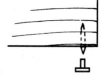

- Another way is to drive a nail in each end. Cut it off and file a point that will enter the benchtop.

- To identify the stones, the ends of the cases may be marked. One, two, or three lines cut with a chisel may be enough. Finish the wood with waterproof varnish.

Materials list

1 piece	$\frac{7}{8} \times 3\frac{5}{8} \times 11$
2 pieces	$\frac{7}{8} \times 3\frac{1}{8} \times 11$
3 pieces	$\frac{7}{8} \times 2\frac{5}{8} \times 11$

Expanding book rack

ONE PROBLEM with putting books on a shelf or in a rack is that if the books do not fill the length, they will not stand upright, and if you cannot get them all in, you do not know what to do with those left out. An expanding rack partly solves the problem. If the books you need on your desk or table vary from time to time, the rack can be adjusted.

This expanding book rack can vary its length from 15 to 26 inches. It is designed for books the size of this volume, but it will hold smaller and larger books. Check the books you want to fit in and alter sizes if necessary.

The important parts are the slides, whose tongues and grooves should be cleanly cut, so use straight-grained hardwood free from flaws for these parts. The ends may be of the same wood, which will take edge decoration without the grain breaking out.

- Prepare the wood for the slides, cutting it too long at first so that you can square the ends after the tongues and grooves have been cut. The bottom and rear slide assemblies are the same. Cut four ¾ × 1½-inch pieces and two ¾-x-2¾-inch pieces.

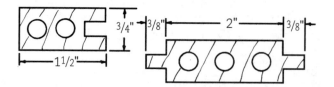

- Cut the tongues and grooves so they will slide together. In the final assembly, the tongues may be waxed for easy movement.

- Make the pair of ends from wood ⅞ inch thick. You may prefer to mark the locations of the slides and prepare the doweled joints before shaping the outsides. As drawn, the books are tilted at 15 degrees to horizontal. The angle can be varied slightly. (See top of page 35.)

- Use the actual slide assemblies to mark positions on the ends. The outside pieces will be doweled to one end and the middle parts of the slides to the other end. (See page 35.)

- Cut the slides 15 inches long and carefully square the ends. The accuracy of the assembly and its appearance depend on this.

- Mark the slide ends for dowels. They may be 5⁄16-inch diameter taken about 1 inch into the slides and ⅝ inch into the ends. Drill the slides and ends.

- Cut the outlines of the ends. Keep the bottom edges flat with a shallow hollow to form feet.

- The exposed edges may be left square or fully rounded, but a shallower rounding looks better. You can cut a molding or multiple beads. (See top of page 36.)

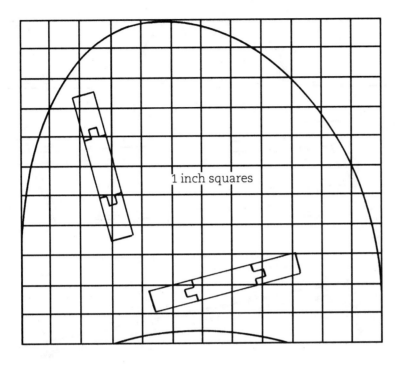

1 inch squares

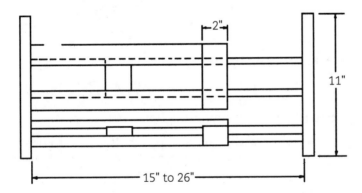

2"

11"

15" to 26"

- Make a stop to fit across the outer slides. This is thin, 2 inches wide, the ends curved to a thinner edge for neatness. (See middle of page 36.)

- Make a similar stop to fit on the central piece. This stop may be glued and pinned on, but do not attach the other one until partial assembly is complete. (See third illustration on page 36.)

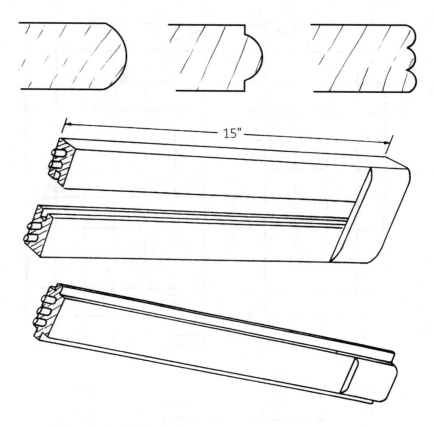

- Dowel and glue the slides to their ends. Allow the glue to set.

- Make a trial assembly of the two sections. Put the long stop across and adjust the spacing of the outer slides as you fit it so the parts move easily throughout their length.

- Finish the wood with stain and polish. It is best to use wax in the moving parts, even if a different polish is used elsewhere.

Materials list

2 ends	⅞ × 11 × 13	
2 slides	¾ × 1½ × 16	
1 slide	¾ × 2¾ × 16	
1 stop	¼ × 2 × 6	
1 stop	¼ × 2 × 3	

Tray

WITH ITS ABILITY to cut moldings accurately and quickly, a router can be used to make both the frame and the base of a tray for use in the kitchen or dining room. Several patterns can be used for the parts of this tray. The base has a butcher block appearance, which can be emphasized by using alternate pieces of different-colored woods. The frame is intended to provide a grip in itself without the addition of handles. Some of the suggested sections are made with pairs of cutters—a molding and its reverse scribe.

Use an attractive hardwood for the frame and two contrasting hardwoods for the base. Sizes are suggested, but any size tray can be made by the same method.

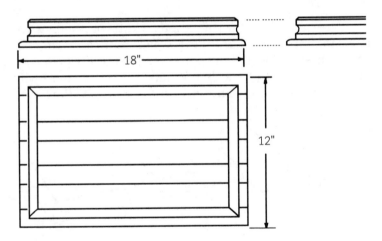

- Prepare the wood for the frame. Although it finishes 1¾ inches × ⅞ inch or 1 inch, it will be easier to hold while using the router if you make it double width with enough at the center for separating by saw or with a straight router cutter. A strip 3¾ inches wide and 30 inches long will make the sides and ends.

- A good basic molding has hollows for fingers and a rounded top. You can use one deeper finger hollow and a matching round at the top. With a small *ovolo* cutter, you can shape both sides of the top, then use its scribe shape to make the hollows. A fully rounded section needs careful blending of the hollows and rounding over the top.

- Cut the pieces to length with mitered ends. Although there is not much strength in plain miters, they will be held close by the screws through the base. Simple glued joints will be sufficient when you assemble the tray if the miters are cut accurately.

- The base can be built up of various widths of ½-inch wood, set in random widths or arranged symmetrically. The arrangement shown alternates 1½-inch strips of one wood with 2-inch strips of another. Whatever arrangement you choose, avoid having joint lines where screws will be used.

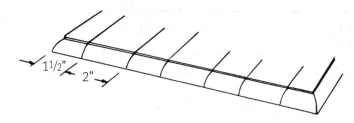

- Edges may simply butt together. With the strength of modern glues, this should be satisfactory, but it is easier to keep the pieces level with another joint. Tongue-and-groove joints are strong. An alternative if you have a suitable pair of *staff bead cutters* uses a rounded tongue and is strong enough.

- Allow for the method of joining when preparing wood for the base. It is easier to keep the parts accurately located if you join the strips in pairs first. When the glue in those joints has set, make the next joints.

- Allow for the base to extend outside the frame enough to add molding to its edges. An extension of ⅝ inch will probably be enough; a wide molding would be inappropriate.

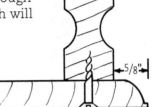

- Cut the base to size and mold the edge using any cutter you choose. The design can match that of the frame.

- Allow for screws upward fairly close to each corner and others at about 5-inch intervals all around. Glue the parts as you screw them.

- Use a clear finish to show the differences in the woods.

- You can use cloth glued over the bottom, or you can put 1-inch-wide strips over the screw heads to provide a nonslip bottom and prevent scratching when the tray is put on a polished surface.

2 frames	⅞ or 1 × 1¾ × 18
2 frames	⅞ or 1 × 1¾ × 12
or both from 2 pieces	⅞ or 1 or 3¾ × 30
4 bases	½ × 1½ × 19
3 bases	½ × 2½ × 19

Materials list

CHAPTER 10

Footstool

A STOOL IS USEFUL around the home for reaching high things or resting the legs or for a child to use as a seat. The stool may be plain and utilitarian, but this one is decorative and has some features of colonial design coupled with adaptations to suit modern equipment, particularly routers.

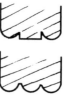

The feet extend to the same size as the top for stability. If the design is altered, do not set the leg ends in much. Early stools would have been painted, and this one can be given a bright color, although a hardwood would look good under a clear finish.

The suggested edge is beading. You may have to alter the wood thickness from ⅞ inch to suit an available cutter; anything between ¹¹⁄₁₆ inch and 1 inch will do. If you have a suitable cutter, there can be three beads. If you only have a single bead cutter, it can be used in both directions to leave a flat center.

Possible sizes are suggested, but you can vary them. Do not make the stool much narrower. A 10-inch height is a reasonable step up and convenient for a child to sit on. (See the top of page 41.)

- Set out the full-size angle of the legs on a piece of scrap plywood and use this as guide to cuts. Set an adjustable bevel to the angle across the legs. (See bottom of page 41.)

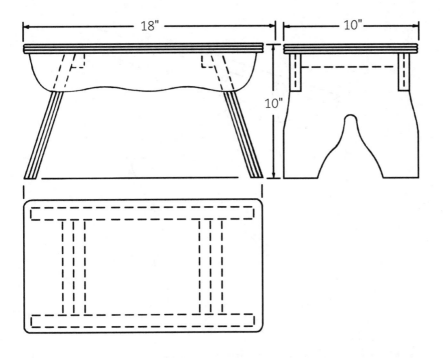

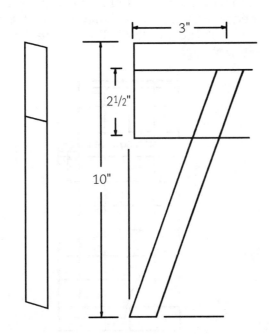

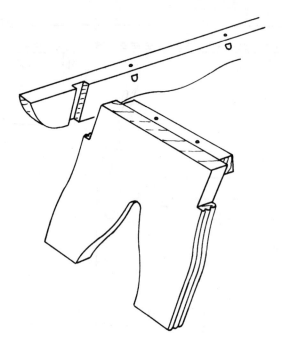

- Mark out the two sides with the angles of the dadoes, which can be cut to half thickness. Round the outlines of the ends. The lower edge between the legs may be left straight or given a wavy outline. Do not cut the hollows more than ¾ inch deep. (See top of page.)

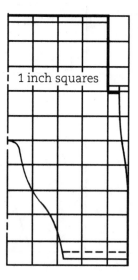

1 inch squares

- Use the squared drawing to mark out the legs. Cut the ends and the notches to suit the angle of each leg and to match the side dadoes. You may have to modify the curve at the top of the cutout to suit the diameter of your cutter. Decorate the exposed edges with beads.

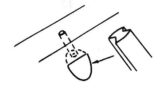

- The top may be held by screws driven downward, but even with counterbored plugged holes, their positions would show. It is better to screw from below. A straight cutter with a diameter of more than that of the screw head is convenient for pocket screwing. Drill diagonally for two or three screws on each side and make pockets to let in the heads.

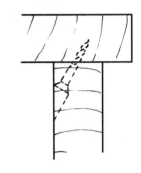

- Assemble the legs and sides. Check that the assembly stands level and is square.

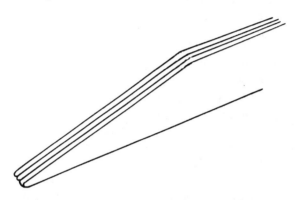

- Make strips to fit inside the tops of the legs. Glue and screw to the legs, and drill for screws upward into the top.

- Make the top overhang ½ inch and round its corners. Cut similar beads to those on the legs all around.

- Invert the lower parts on the underside of the top; glue and screw together.

- Finish with paint or varnish, but avoid making the top slippery.

Materials list

2 legs	⅞ × 10 × 11
2 sides	⅞ × 2½ × 18
1 top	⅞ × 10 × 19
2 top strips	1 × 1 × 10

CHAPTER 11

Mirror on stand

A MIRROR that swings on a stand with two small drawers may be used in a bedroom or the mirror alone attached to a wall.

Because a router can follow curves as easily as straight lines, there can be some shaping in the frame, although this item uses a rectangular mirror about 11 × 15 inches. The size can be adjusted, so you may be able to avoid having glass specially cut by using a standard mirror.

It would be advisable to use a close-grained hardwood to reduce the risk of grain breaking out when molding edges or cutting joints. Start with the mirror frame; then other sizes can be adjusted slightly to suit it. (See top of page 45.)

The section of frame suggested is 1¼ × 1¼ inches, with a wider piece for the top, but you may have to adjust sizes to suit your router cutters. You need a pair of cutters to make the molding and a scribes to fit it. (See second illustration on page 45.)

The rabbet will probably have to be cut with a separate cutter. Into the ½-inch rabbet you must fit the glass and a fillet to hold it in place. (See third illustration on page 45.) Edges are molded, then the parts scribed together at the corners. (See the top of page 46.) Decide on your suitable cutters and vary the section of wood to suit them. These instructions assume you are using 1¼-inch-square wood.

To make the mirror frame, prepare sufficient wood for the sides and bottom rail. Mold and rabbet the inner edges.

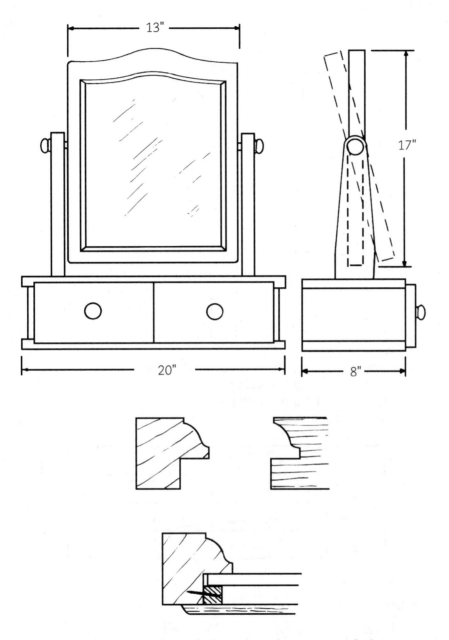

- Although the top is shaped, the mirror is set squarely into a rabbet. Start with a piece of 1¼-inch wood 3½ inches wide and cut a rabbet the same depth as the other rabbets but 1½ inches wide. (See second illustration on the next page.)

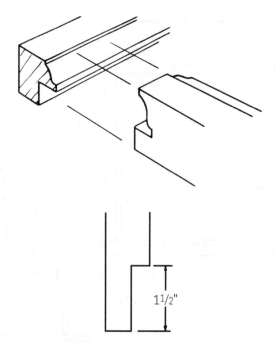

1¹/₂"

- Using the squared drawing, draw the shape of the frame top. At the center there should be ½ inch of the rabbet remaining; at the sides, the outer curve should not come closer than ⅝ inch to the corner of the glass.

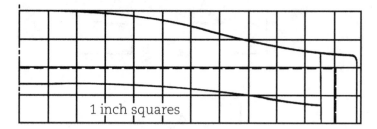

1 inch squares

- Cut the inner and outer curves. Mold the inner edge.

- Check the size of the glass. When the frame is assembled, there can be about ¹/₁₆-inch clearance all round the edges in the rabbets.

- Cut the scribed ends of the top and bottom rails. Mark the sides where these rails will fit. Assemble the frame, clamping tightly, facedown. Reinforce the corner glue joints with fine screws driven from the back through the tongues in the rabbets. They will be hidden by the back. Cut off any extending ends and round the corners.

- If the mirror in its frame will be used alone, finish the wood with stain and polish. Cut fillets to hold the mirror. Fit them with pins at fairly wide intervals so that they are easily removed if you have to replace the glass.

- Make a back from thin plywood or hardboard. Round its edges and fasten it to the frame with small screws. The back is shown on the surface, but it could be let into a second rabbet if you allow extra thickness in the frame.

- The front of the frame may be further decorated with a bead or molding worked around its outer edge, but excess decoration should be avoided. It will probably be sufficient to round the outer edges and corners lightly.

- You can put the mirror on a stand with just the two parts and a base, shown as the top of a block of two drawers. Construction is the same, but it would be advisable to make the base thicker than the ¾ inch of the stand with drawers.

- The frame pivots on screws just above its center. If you use a mirror of another size, arrange the pivot up to 1 inch above the middle and allow about 1-inch clearance below.

- The posts are 1 inch thick and 3 inches wide at the bottom. Taper to 2-inch rounded tops. Allow for tenons at the bottom. Decorate the edges by rounding or with beads. (Shown here.)

- The pivots are stout screws in deeply counterbored holes. Fiber, leather, or rubber washers provide friction to hold the mirror at any angle. The screw heads are hidden under wooden knobs, which are pressed in so they can be pulled out if you ever need to adjust the screws. You can turn your own knobs, but suitable ones are sold as drawer pulls. (See the top of next page.)

- The mortises in the base may be cut with a router cutter, then the tenons shaped to fit. A suitable size would be ¾ inch wide and 2½ inches long. (See second illustration on page 48.)

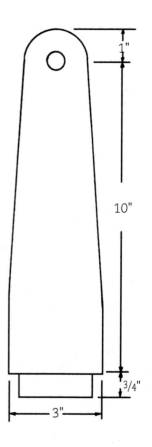

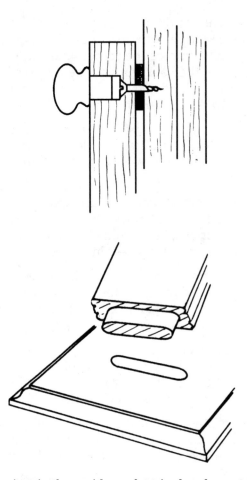

- The base is 8 inches wide and 20 inches long. Measure the width across the frame, washers, and posts to get the correct spacing so that the posts will be upright. Mark and cut the mortise-and-tenon joints.

- The edges of the base should be molded, preferably matching the design used in the mirror frame. If you intend to complete the stand with drawers, leave the edges until later. Otherwise, mold the base and assemble the posts to it. If necessary, the tenons can be tightened by wedges driven into saw cuts from below. Check that the posts stand upright and try the action of the mirror before disassembling for finishing.

- The base may be completed with one or two drawers. For one wide drawer, leave out the center partition. Make the top of the block of drawers, as described above, as a base and cut another piece without the mortises for the bottom.

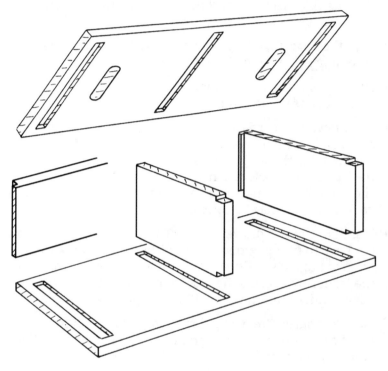

- Cut the three upright parts with the grain vertical. The two outer pieces are the same width as the long parts, but the partition is reduced to allow the back to fit across. The height may be as you wish, but drawers 4 inches high will be a useful size and make a stand with attractive proportions.

- Make rabbets in the top and bottom parts to within ¾ inch of front and rear edges. Cut the outer upright to fit. The partition will fit at the back without notching. The joints are shown with squared ends. The routered grooves can be trimmed with a chisel, or leave the grooves with rounded ends and shape the other piece to fit. The amount of hand work is about the same whichever method you choose.

- Cut grooves in the rear edges of the end uprights to take tongues on the back.

- Mold all around the top piece as described for an independent base, but do not take the molding deeper than half the thickness or it will be covered by the drawer fronts. Mold the ends of the bottom only.

- Glue the parts together. Clamp tightly. The back will hold the assembly square, but check that there is no twist.

- Fit the posts. Check that they are upright and that the ends of the tenons do not project into the drawer spaces.

- The drawers may be made with dovetail joints, but in this small size it should be satisfactory to use tight-fitting grooves reinforced with pins if necessary. The drawer fronts overlap the front of the base and meet over the partition. The fronts should be of the same wood as the rest of the stand, but the back and sides may be softwood.

- Mark out the two drawer fronts. The drawer sides are shown cut back to fit into grooves in the front. Mark the width on the front to allow a little clearance in the compartment. If the front is to overlap the block top and bottom, it will be ¾ inch wider than the sides. (Shown opposite.)

- Make the sides. Groove the lower edges to take ⅛-inch hardboard or plywood and groove for the back, which fits above the bottom.

- Make the back, using the layout of the front as a guide to its length.

- Mold all around the edges of the drawer front. If you prefer, the meeting edges of the two fronts may be left square.

- Glue and pin a small strip on the front to support the front edge of the drawer bottom.

- Assemble the drawer parts without the bottom. Try them in position; make any adjustment necessary by planing edges. When you are satisfied, slide in the bottom and check that the drawer still slides correctly. Screw upward through the bottom into the back. There is no need to use glue, except where the bottom rests on the front strip.

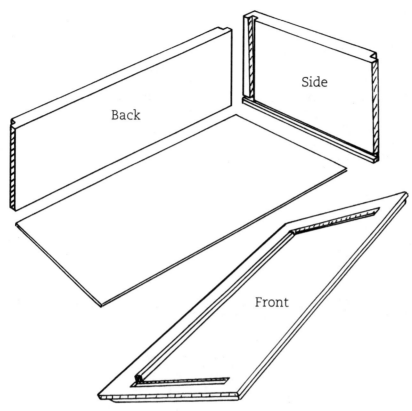

Back

Side

Front

- Fit drawer handles. Round knobs will match those over the mirror pivots.

- Finish with stain and polish. The underside may be covered with cloth either all over or only as strips near the edge.

2 mirror sides	1¼ × 1¼ × 17
1 mirror bottom	1¼ × 1¼ × 13
1 mirror top	1¼ × 3½ × 13
1 mirror back	13 × 17 × ⅛ (plywood)
2 fillets	⁵⁄₁₆ × ⁵⁄₁₆ × 16
2 fillets	⁵⁄₁₆ × ⁵⁄₁₆ × 12
2 posts	1 × 3 × 13
1 drawer block top	¾ × 8 × 21
1 drawer block bottom	¾ × 8 × 21
2 drawer block ends	¾ × 8 × 6

Materials list

1 drawer block partition	¾ × 7¼ × 6
1 drawer block back	¾ × 4 × 21
2 drawer fronts	¾ × 4¾ × 11
2 drawer backs	½ × 3½ × 11
4 drawer sides	½ × 4 × 8
2 drawer bottoms	8 × 10 × ⅛ (plywood)
2 bottom fillets	¼ × ¼ × 10

Corner shelves

CHAPTER
12

SHELVES IN THE corner of a room will fill a space that may not otherwise be used and will provide a place to display small souvenirs and other items. This block of three shelves is a reasonable size for most situations, but the design can be modified to anything from a two-shelf arrangement to floor to ceiling.

The sizes shown are intended for solid wood. You can use plywood or particleboard for the greater part with solid wood edging attached by tongue-and-groove joints.

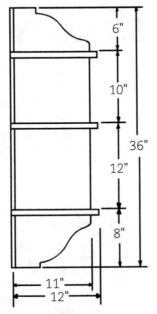

Before starting construction, check the angle of the corner of the room. It should be 90 degrees, but it may be a few degrees out, and that affects the fit of the shelves. Set an adjustable bevel to the angle of the corner and use that instead of a square when marking.

• The two sides are a pair, except that one has a rabbet to take the other. Make one side narrower by the amount left on the other piece.

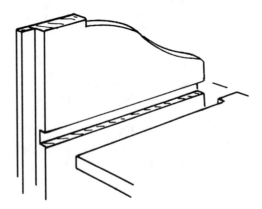

- Mark the dadoes for the shelves and draw the shapes for top and bottom. Do not cut to shape yet.

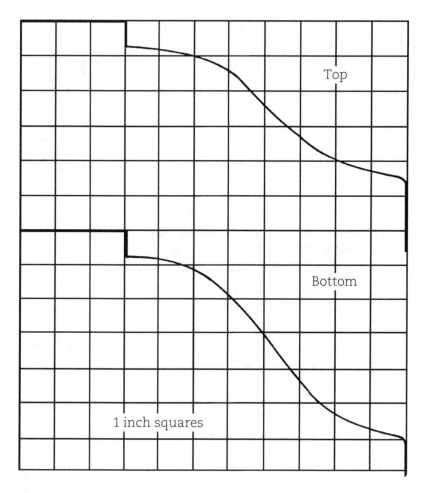

Top

Bottom

1 inch squares

- The three shelves are identical. Lay the grain parallel with the front edges. Cut the dadoes for them in the sides, then notch them so that their ends will touch the wall. Round the outer corners. (See far right.)

- Cut the shapes at the tops and bottoms of the ends.

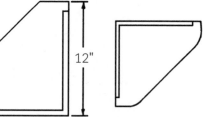

Corner shelves   55

- You can decorate the edges—perhaps on the shelf edges only, the side edges left square. The straight parts of the sides may be molded or decoration carried around the ends.

- Shelf edges may have just a central bead, or you can use a reverse cutter to make a central flute. The shelf edges may be fully beaded, carried around wall to wall. The side edges may also be fully beaded, or you can run a single bead along the inward-facing corners. This might be arranged to face along the wall or inward. It is advisable to try the molding bits you have on scrapwood first to decide which to use.

- Since the back surfaces will be hidden, all joints may be screwed in and glued. Drill for screws through the sides before assembly. See that the joints pull tight, especially the front corners of the shelves where gaps will be particularly obvious.

- Hanging screws can be located fairly close under the top shelf where they will not show. They take the weight, but two more under the bottom shelf will hold the shelves tight to the wall.

- Finish with stain and polish. With this screwed assembly, you can finish all parts except surfaces that will be glued, before bringing them together.

Materials list

| 2 sides | ⅝ × 11 × 37 |
| 3 shelves | ⅝ × 11 × 18 |

Molded box

A BOX WITH AN overhanging top and bottom provides an opportunity to use router cutters for joints and decoration. The box can be any size, from a tiny one for jewelry to a blanket chest; construction techniques are basically the same. To a certain extent, the size will depend on your bits. If they suit wood of ¾-inch thickness, they can't make a small box, but they can make a box of seat height for storage in a bedroom. The example, a small box for a table or dresser, is made of ½-inch wood, preferably an attractive hardwood so grain markings will improve appearance.

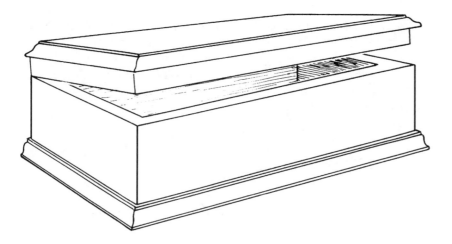

The sides and ends of the body and the lid are first made in one piece, then sawn apart along the dividing line. If this is done with a fine saw with the wood against a brace so that the saw blade does not wander, you need do very little to smooth the edges, and the total depth will be reduced only slightly. If you expect to remove much wood after sawing, draw parallel lines about ⅛ inch apart and saw between them, then use the lines as guides when leveling the edges.

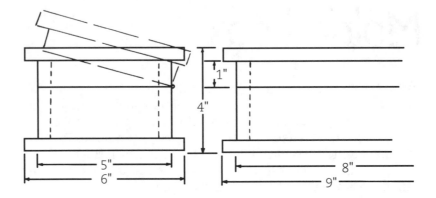

- Prepare the wood for the sides and ends. Mark out the lengths, leaving a little extra wood outside the marked lines until the method of joining is decided.

- Several corner joints are possible. A simple overlap with nails or screws would suit a utilitarian construction, but something better is advisable. If you have suitable cutters, *dovetails* are strong and will give the box character. Finger joints are just as strong, but their appearance is not as attractive.

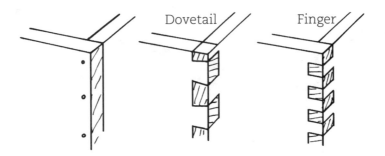

If end grain is not to show at the corners, you must use miters at the outside. A simple miter is not very strong because glue does not hold well on end grain, but for a small box this might still be satisfactory. An improvement is to notch one piece into the other. In both cases, a few pins can be driven through the joints with their heads set in and covered with stopping. (See top of page 59.)

Some cutters can make interlocking miter joints. Take care when cutting and fitting cross-grained pieces. This is easier if the interlocking parts are tapered.

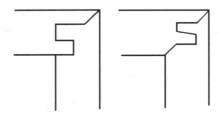

- Join the corners. Level the outsides if necessary.

- Separate the lid from the box. Mark the adjoining hinged sides so the two parts will match.

- Notch the edges for hinges, which may be 2 inches long on a box of the size suggested. Make a temporary assembly with a few screws to test that the two parts come together correctly. Remove the hinges until the top and bottom have been fitted.

- Cut the top and bottom to overlap ½ inch all around.

- How you decorate the edges will depend on available cutters and your preferences. For most patterns, a slightly wider molding on the top edges than on the bottom will look best. The two moldings need not have the same form, although a resemblance is advisable. At the bottom, leave about ⅛ inch flat outside the sides and ends.

An *ovolo* or a classic molding, both the same width or with the top one wider, may be used. Round the lower edges of the top. Multiple beads can be used in a similar way.

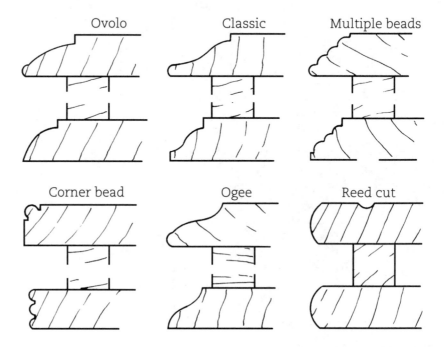

The bottom edge may be fully beaded and the lid treated in a similar way or given one corner bead. An *ogee* molding may be used, possibly with a bead on the lid edge. A simple rounding may have a *reed cut* on the top.

- Glue the top and bottom in place. In a larger box, it is advisable also to use screws through the bottom and some pins with countersunk heads through the top. Fill in with wood filler.

- Fit the hinges and test the fit and action of the parts.

- Because a small box might be lifted by its lid, some sort of fastener is advisable; a lock or a small hook and eye.

- Finish the box with stain and polish. Cloth may be glued underneath.

Materials list

2 sides	½ × 3 × 9	
2 ends	½ × 3 × 6	
1 top	½ × 6 × 11	
1 bottom	½ × 6 × 11	

Tambour box

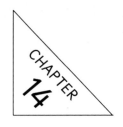

YOU CAN MAKE a box lid that slides out of the way but has a pleasing appearance when closed, by routing grooves into which strips glued to canvas can move. Such a box is shown 18 inches long and about 6 inches wide and high. It can store equipment on a desk, hold jewelry on a dresser, hold cutlery and other things in the kitchen. You can use the same method of construction for boxes of other sizes.

A disappearing lid made of wood strips glued to canvas is called a *tambour fall*. In this case, the lid closes with a handle; when it is pushed back, the strips are guided by grooves in the sides to go behind and below an internal end and bottom.

The thin strips that make the tambour lid should be straight-grained to reduce the risk of warping. Use hardwood throughout, but the lid parts need not be the same wood as the box. Wood of a contrasting color might improve appearance.

The main parts are joined with glued dado joints. You do not need to add pins or screws to them, but the bottom is best screwed on. Suggested sizes are shown. The key sizes and cuts are the grooves in opposite sides to take the sliding tambour ends. Other sizes may have to be modified slightly after these grooves are cut. (See top of page 62.)

There are dado grooves in the sides for all crosswise parts except the narrow top at the rear end, which will fit between the sides and be glued to them and the top edge of the back. Visualize the parts, how they will assemble, and how the lid must slide before marking and cutting wood. (See second illustration on page 62.)

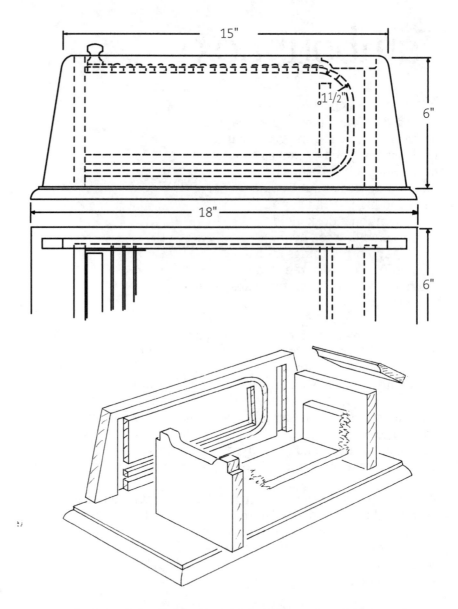

- Mark out a pair of opposite sides and see that they match. Cut the grooves for the lid ends ¼ inch wide and ¼ inch deep. Do not make the curves too small a radius or the lid might stick; a 1½-inch radius should be satisfactory. It is important that these grooves are smooth. You might need to rub inside with folded abrasive paper.

- Cut the other grooves, checking them against the thickness of the wood to be fitted into them. The grooves for the two outer box ends are stopped ⅜ inch from the top edges. Arrange the grooves for the inner bottom and end so they have sufficient clearance from the curves of the tambour grooves. You can use plywood for the inner parts if you do not want to use solid wood.

- Make the outer back crosspiece to reach to the top of its stopped grooves. Use it as a guide for the lengths of other crosswise pieces. Notch the outer front at the grooves so it comes level with the tops of the sides. Cut down the center of its top edge to give clearance to grip the handle. Make the inner bottom and end to match the width of the other parts.

- Cut the rear top piece with a chamfer or hollow so it will easily clear the sliding lid. Make this a little oversize in width and length for accurate fitting after the other parts are assembled.

- The tambour lid is shown with a piece under the handle 1 inch wide and twenty-two other strips ½ inch wide. It will not matter if your wood is slightly wider or narrower, but you need sufficient pieces to leave something under the rear top piece when the lid is closed. Strips much wider might not pass easily around the curved slots.

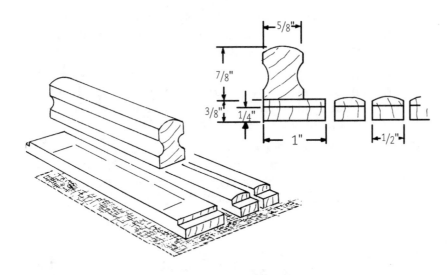

- Leave the edges of the piece under the handle square, but round the top edges of the narrow strips. Cut so that the ends will have a little clearance in the grooves. Cut down the ends to a thickness that will slide in the grooves. The curved parts of the grooves are the controlling points when trying fits. You can lightly bevel the undersides of the strip ends.

- Use your own ideas for a handle, but a simple section is shown. If you use a different form, remember that it must move both ways. Glue it in place.

- You need canvas or stout cloth without noticeable stretch for the underside of the tambour fall. Cut it to a width that will pass easily between the assembled sides. It must be clear of the grooves. Avoid canvas that has been treated with waterproofing solution; it might not accept glue.

- You should be able to use ordinary wood glue to join the strips, but you might prefer an impact adhesive. If you have doubts, experiment with scrap materials.

- Take care to assemble the lid squarely. Use sufficient glue, but try to avoid getting any between the strips. Leave the assembly under pressure while the glue sets, but when it has hardened to the stage where you can handle it, lift the tambour carefully and flex it so you can scrape off any glue that has oozed between the parts.

- Apply a brushed finish to the tambour lid. In the finished box, the tambour is visible only flat, so you do not need to carry the finish down the sides of the strips.

- Join all the crosspieces to one side and check squareness. Be careful not to get glue in the lid groove. Insert the lid and join on the second side. Check lid movement and leave the assembly for the glue to set fully.

- Make the bottom to extend sufficiently for a molded edge. Drill for screws, countersunk enough to keep the heads clear of a tabletop. You will probably find it convenient to apply a finish before screwing on the bottom.

Materials list		
2 sides	$\frac{5}{8} \times 6 \times 18$	
1 outer end	$\frac{5}{8} \times 6 \times 6$	
1 outer end	$\frac{5}{8} \times 5\frac{3}{8} \times 6$	

1 bottom   ⅝ × 6 × 19
1 inner end   ⅜ × 3¼ × 6
1 inner bottom   ⅜ × 6 × 12
1 lid strip   ⅜ × 1 × 6
22 lid strips   ⅜ × ½ × 6
1 handle   ⅝ × ⅞ × 5

CHAPTER 15

Drop-leaf side table

A NARROW TABLETOP can be widened with one or two hinged flaps. In its simplest form, the square edges of the flap and top have plain hinges. This leaves an ugly gap when the flap is down, although the arrangement functions well. A better appearance results if the meeting edges are molded to match and the table's other edges are given a similar molding. Without a router, cutting these moldings may be tedious and the mating edges difficult to fit, but suitable bits in a router ensure accuracy, and the shapes are easy to cut, even on a curved outline.

The traditional molding for the meeting edges of top and flap is an ovolo on the table edge and a matching reverse cut on the flap. With these go *backflap hinges*, which are let in with the knuckles upward. One hinge arm is long enough to bridge the gap in the flap. The center of the knuckle has to be located at the center of the curve of the ovolo so that when the flap swings down, the molded edge fills the gap. When the flap is up, the joint closes. If the outer edges of the top and flap also have ovolo moldings, the appearance is the same all around.

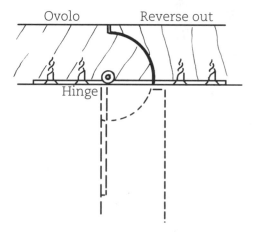

Although the ovolo section is usual, you can use other matched moldings, particularly where a single cutter can be reversed. You may experiment on scrapwood with router cutters to produce different joints and edges.

This project is a side table with one flap. When closed, the tabletop projects about 15 inches from the wall. When the flap is raised, the top is increased to about 30 inches. The table is shown with a semicircular flap, but a narrower flap can be semielliptical or parallel with rounded corners if the space you have for the table allows less than 30 inches from the wall.

Any wood may be used. The top flap may have to be built up by gluing pieces together. Choose fully seasoned wood, preferably quartersawn, so the risk of the flap warping is reduced.

If you modify sizes, note that the gate leg has to open to near the center of the edge of the flap and that there must be space for it to close between the table legs and leave space for the flap to drop. (See top of page 68.)

- Start by marking out the five legs together to get lengths, joint positions, and decorations matching. Leave a little extra at the top of each leg until after the joints are cut. The gate leg is the same as the others, except the rails meet one surface only. (See margin of next page.)

- The top rails will have double tenons, and the lower rails a single tenon. The mortises may be ½ inch wide, but make them to suit your cutters. Take the mortises in to meet in the legs. (See top of page 69.)

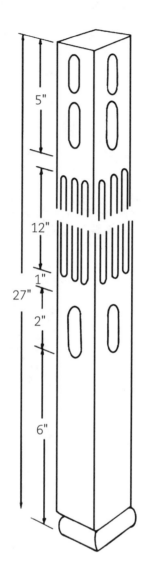

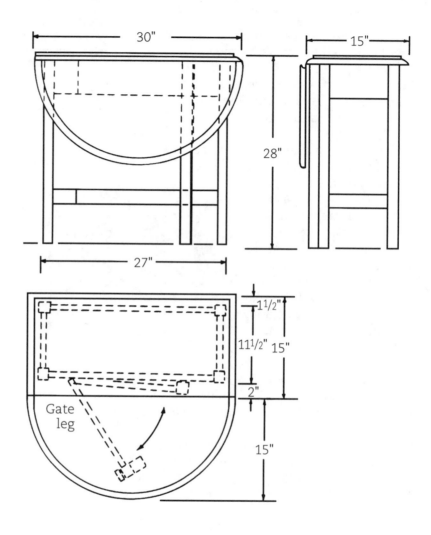

Gate
leg

- Mark out the top and bottom table rails together to give a finished size of 11½ inches over the legs with tenons rounded to match the mortises. Groove the top rails for buttons. (See second illustration on page 69.)

- For the gate, make rails with tenons at one end.

- Make feet at the bottoms of the legs by cutting beads all around.

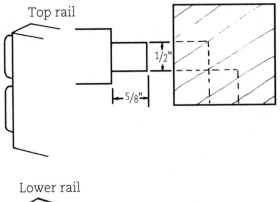

Top rail

1/2"

5/8"

Lower rail

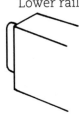

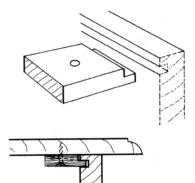

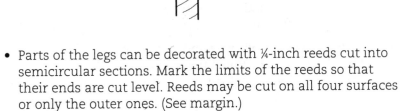

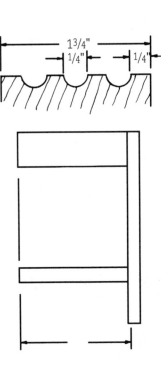

1 3/4"

1/4"

1/4"

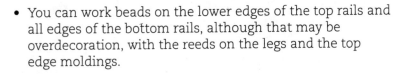

- Parts of the legs can be decorated with ¼-inch reeds cut into semicircular sections. Mark the limits of the reeds so that their ends are cut level. Reeds may be cut on all four surfaces or only the outer ones. (See margin.)

- You can work beads on the lower edges of the top rails and all edges of the bottom rails, although that may be overdecoration, with the reeds on the legs and the top edge moldings.

Drop-leaf side table   69

- Assemble the table parts. Put together opposite long sides and check that they are square and matching, then join in the short rails. See that the assembly is square and stands level.

- Join the gate rails to their leg, checking accuracy against the spacing of the table side. Fit hinges to the ends of the gate rails, but do not attach them to the table rails yet.

- Cut the tabletop to size and shape the flap. Cut the matching moldings along their meeting edges. Let in three or four backflap hinges and test the action of the joint.

- If necessary, trim the edges of the top and flap so that they match when the flap is up. Cut the molding all around the top and flap while these parts are joined, then remove the hinges until you have done other work.

- Make buttons to attach the top, one at each end and two along each side. Invert the framework on the underside of the top and screw on the buttons. The top should have more overhang on the hinged side to give clearance for the gate leg to fold. The overhang at the other side should be enough to allow the legs to clear the room's baseboard.

- While the table is still inverted, join the flap with the backflap hinges. Mark where the gate leg is to come. Try the gate in this position and swing it into the table rail to obtain the positions of the hinges. The gate leg may rub under the flap as it is pulled out, but it will be better to put a stop under the flap, then cut down the top edge of the leg and rail to allow for this so the opened gate closes onto the stop. Glue the stop under the flap. Screw the gate hinges to the table rails.

- Turn the table the right way and test the opening and closing action. If satisfactory, finish the wood to match the surroundings or nearby furniture.

Materials list

5 legs	1¾ × 1¾ × 28	
2 rails	1 × 5 × 27	
2 rails	1 × 2 × 27	

2 rails	$1 \times 5 \times 12$
2 rails	$1 \times 2 \times 12$
1 rail	$1 \times 5 \times 17$
1 rail	$1 \times 2 \times 17$
2 tops	$1 \times 15 \times 31$

CHAPTER 16

Mirror-front bathroom cabinet

A CUPBOARD with a shelf and a door including a mirror can hold many small things in a bathroom.

A router will cut the joints and make the moldings on edges and around the mirror.

This cabinet may be altered to suit your router bits or the size of a standard mirror. The suggested sizes are based on a mirror frame of wood 1 inch thick and 1½ inches wide using a molding ⅜ inch deep on the front edge. The mirror and its retaining fillets fit into a deep rabbet, and the thin plywood or hardboard back goes into a wider rabbet. You may have to make the frame sections in stages, the rabbets cut separately from the molding. You must be able to make the scribing cuts on the ends of the rails. Check your available cutters and adjust the frame section to suit. The instructions assume you can make the sections suggested.

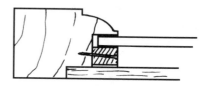

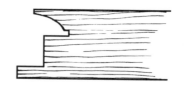

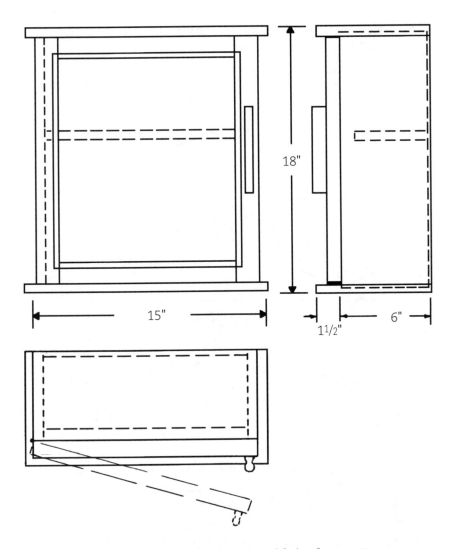

- If you already have the mirror, start with its frame. You may have to modify the cabinet size slightly to allow for the finished size of the door.

- Make the mirror-frame molding, leaving the stiles a little too long so the ends can be trimmed to the rails after assembly.

- Allow a little clearance around the mirror and cut the scribed ends of the rails. Mark where they will come on the stiles.

- Assemble the door, using the mirror to check size and squareness before the glue sets.

- Trim the outside, cut the fillets that will hold the glass, and make the back to fit into its rabbet. Try a dry assembly, but do not mount the parts permanently yet.

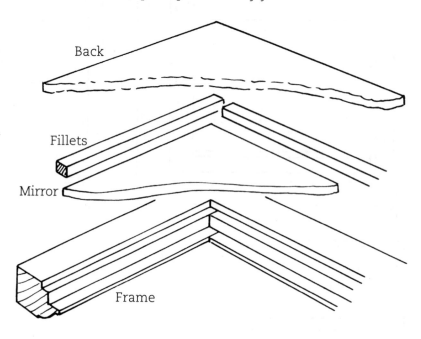

- The door will overlap the two cabinet sides but come between the top and bottom. Check its sizes and allow a little clearance at top and bottom when deciding on the sizes of other parts.

- Top and bottom are the same. Allow for the thickness of the door, with a further ½-inch projection forward and ⅜-inch projection at each side. Cut dadoes for the sides and a rabbet for the back.

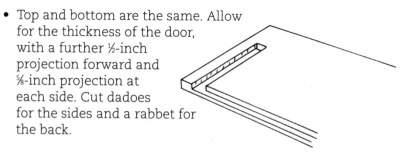

- Make the pair of sides with rabbets for the back. Allow for a shelf 5 inches wide at a height to suit the intended contents. Its front can be rounded to suit the dado ends. There may be more than one shelf, and you may wish to cut slots or holes in them to take glasses, brushes, and so on.

- The extending ends and fronts of the top and bottom may be rounded or molded. In any case, lightly round the front corners.

- Assemble the parts of the cabinet. Glue-in the back, with a few pins or fine nails. If the dado joints need strengthening, use a few fine nails from outside with their heads set below the surface and covered with wood filler.

- Notch one cabinet side for 2-inch hinges.

- Fit a handle to one side of the door. This can be a metal knob, but a molded strip can be made and held with screws from behind. A 6-inch handle is easy to find if you have to feel for it with soap-filled eyes. Try the door and hinges in position.

- Finish the wood with varnish or paint.

- Secure the mirror with a few pins through the fillets. Fit the door back without glue in case you have to remove the mirror. Drive screws or fine nails through it into its rabbet.

- Fit a spring or magnetic catch. Mount the cabinet to the wall with screws through the back.

Materials list

2 door stiles	$1 \times 1\frac{1}{2} \times 18$
2 door rails	$1 \times 1\frac{1}{2} \times 15$
1 door back	$13 \times 16 \times \frac{3}{16}$ (plywood)
2 fillets	$\frac{1}{4} \times \frac{3}{8} \times 16$
2 fillets	$\frac{1}{4} \times \frac{3}{8} \times 13$
1 top	$\frac{5}{8} \times 7\frac{1}{2} \times 17$
1 bottom	$\frac{5}{8} \times 7\frac{1}{2} \times 17$
2 sides	$\frac{5}{8} \times 6 \times 18$
1 shelf	$\frac{5}{8} \times 5 \times 15$
1 back	$15 \times 17 \times \frac{3}{16}$ (plywood)
1 handle	$\frac{5}{8} \times 1 \times 7$

Mirror-front bathroom cabinet 75

CHAPTER 17

Chest of drawers

IN MAKING A block of drawers, most of the joints and decoration can be done with a router. The drawers can be any size, from a small unit to store a collection of fossils to a large chest for blankets and clothing. The method of construction is basically the same, whatever the size. The chest used as an example is a moderate size for use in a bedroom.

If you alter the size, there are a few design points to observe. If the length and height of drawers vary, the effect is more pleasing than if they are about the same. Drawers should decrease in height depth toward the top. Handles should be set above the halfway position on each drawer.

For a painted finish, you can use any wood, but if the chest is to be polished, all the external parts should be of a good hardwood. Drawer parts, except for the fronts, might be of a cheaper wood. Drawer bottoms and the chest back may be thin plywood or hardboard. Most structural parts are ⅞ inch thick. The chest has three drawers under a molded top and over a *plinth*. Pieces may have to be glued together to make up the widths for the top and ends.

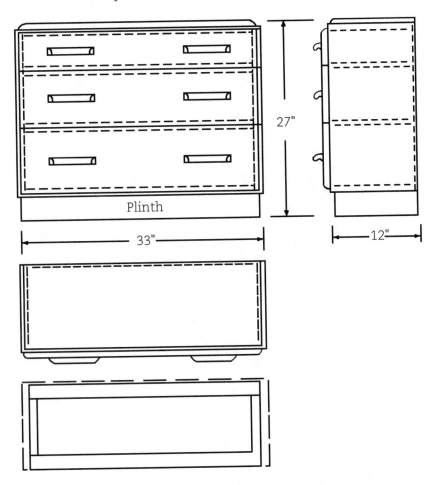

- Mark out the pair of ends with a rabbet for the back. Keep the rabbet less than half the thickness of the wood so the back will be hidden by the top. Mark the positions of the dividers on the ends. (See top of next page.)

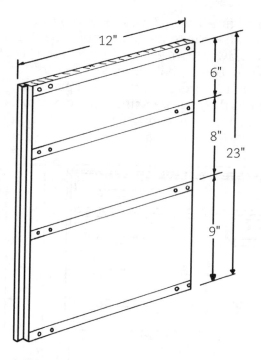

- Four identical frames make up the top, bottom, and drawer divisions. Only the front edge will show, so cheaper wood may be used inside. Each frame comes level with the sides at the front and against the plywood back.

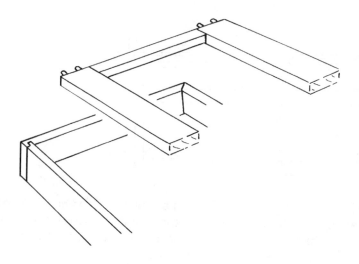

- The 2-inch strips are joined with ⅞-inch-square pieces and must be kept level for smooth running of the drawers, so notch them together. Drill for ⅜-inch dowels. Assemble the frames and see that they match and are square.

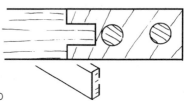

- Join the frames to the ends and fit the back temporarily to keep the assembly square. You may wish to remove it later to get at the backs of the drawers when fitting them.

- The plinth is a frame set back ⅞ inch at the sides and front but level at the back. A depth of 3 inches should be satisfactory. Where it shows at the front, the corners should be mitered, using any of the router joints. If you choose a plain miter, it may be strengthened with a block glued inside. At the back, the sides can overlap the rear piece with a dado joint.

- At the front and back, screw downward into the plinth through the bottom rail. Do the same at the sides, but since the overlap is not very much, drive the screws diagonally.

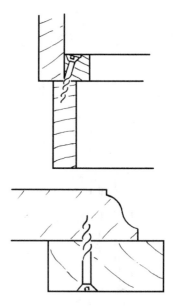

- Make the top level at the back and set back ⅞₆ inch at front and ends. Mold its front and ends. This can be any section for which you have a cutter, but do not make it very wide. Attach the top with glue and screws through the top frame.

- The drawers are intended to run with their bottom edges on the frames. If you wish to fit metal or plastic runners, make the bodies of the drawers narrower to suit. The drawer fronts overlap the frames to the midthickness around the case edges and meet along the centers of the dividing rails. Outer edges are molded to match the top. (See top of page 80.)

- Make the three pairs of drawer sides. Each side should slide easily in its space. Make the lengths to come within about ¼ inch of the chest back and allow enough at the front to fit into dadoes. Groove the lower edges for the bottoms and cut dadoes to take the backs, which will fit around the bottom.

- Make the drawer fronts the same length, reaching halfway over the chest ends and wide enough almost to meet.

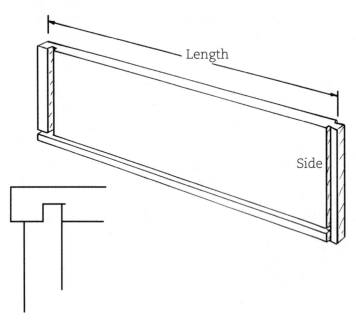

Length

Side

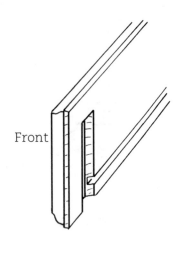

Front

- Cut dado joints between the drawer sides and fronts, preferably with a dovetail section. The dadoes stop to allow the fronts to overlap the rails. At the bottoms, the groove will run through a little below the sides, but in normal use that will not show.

- Cut grooves in the drawer fronts to take the bottoms, allowing for the overhang of the front lower edges.

- Mold the ends of all drawer fronts, the top edge of the top drawer, and the bottom edge of the bottom drawer.

- Make the drawer backs. Be careful that they do not stand higher than the sides.

- Assemble the drawers without their bottoms and test their action. If this is satisfactory, slide in the bottoms and screw up into the backs. Fit the chest back permanently.

- The drawer handles may be metal or plastic, or you can make wooden ones. A possible section is shown. This could be routered in a sufficient length for all the handles on the edge of a wider board, then cut off. The ends may be rounded or cut at an angle. Fix them with glue and screws from inside the drawers.

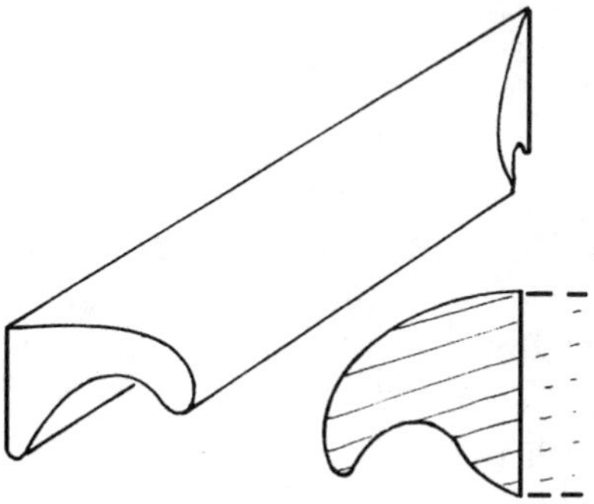

- Finish with polish or paint. Wax on the edges of the drawer sides will give a smooth action.

Materials list

2 sides	⅞ × 12 × 24
1 top	⅞ × 11⅛ × 33
8 frames	⅞ × 2 × 33
8 frames	⅞ × ⅞ × 12
2 plinths	⅞ × 3 × 33
2 plinths	⅞ × 3 × 12
1 drawer front	⅞ × 6 × 33
1 drawer front	⅞ × 8 × 33
1 drawer front	⅞ × 9 × 33
2 drawer sides	⅝ × 5⅛ × 13
2 drawer sides	⅝ × 7 1/18 × 13
2 drawer sides	⅝ × 7¼ × 13
1 drawer back	⅝ × 4⅝ × 33
1 drawer back	⅝ × 6⅝ × 33
1 drawer back	⅝ × 6¾ × 33
6 drawer handles	1¼ × 1¼ × 6
3 drawer bottoms	12 × 32 × ¼ (plywood)
1 chest back	23 × 33 × ¼ (plywood)

CHAPTER 18

Doors

Wıтн suiтаble router cutters, you can make a variety of doors, particularly paneled types, many of which would be difficult if not impossible to make by other means. You can make doors varying in size and patterns, from plain functional ones to elaborate decorative ones. The paneled construction is suitable for doors of kitchen and bathroom cabinets, but you can make large doors or small doors in the same way.

It is advisable to follow traditional construction—the panel let into grooves in a solid wood frame and the upright parts of the frame going to the full height, with horizontal members joined to them with mortise-and-tenon joints. In some instances you can use dowels instead of mortise-and-tenon. If the panel is plywood or another man-made board, it will not expand and contract, and it can be fixed in its grooves. A solid-wood panel can vary in width across its grain as it gives up or takes in moisture because of variations in humidity, so the grooves should be deep enough for the loose panel to expand and contract; otherwise, if it is secured tightly at its edges, there can be distortion or cracking.

Because of an optical effect, it is usual to make a doorframe with its bottom rail wider than the sides and top. If it is made the same width, it will appear narrower.

For a basic plywood-paneled door, you can make the grooved frame parts without decoration. At the corners, the tenons should be about one-third the thickness of the wood, which will probably be more than the width of the grooves. You can take the tenons right through or cut them short, depending on the thickness of the wood and whether you want the door edges to appear uncut.

- Cut back the width of the tenon to the bottom of the groove and allow a small amount of solid wood outside the mortise. Make a haunch there to fill the depth of the groove. Cut the mortise to match the tenon. Leave a short length of waste wood outside each mortised end until after assembly. This reduces the risk of breaking out as you cut the mortise and protects the corner until the door is finished.

- You can decorate this type of doorframe with a simple chamfer or rounding on one or both inner edges. At a corner, you have to arrange for the meeting of the decorations, usually with a miter. Cut back to the base of the groove on the piece to be mortised. It looks best if you make the chamfer or rounding the same width as the depth of the groove. Cut back the width of the tenon a similar amount. Miter the projecting parts of each piece to meet closely. Reduce the width of the tenon at its outer edge and cut a mortise to match.

- You can use dowels at this type of corner instead of a tenon. Have at least two dowels of ample size and drill at least as much as three times their diameter into each part. Cut back and miter the inner edges in a similar way to the mortise-and-tenon corner.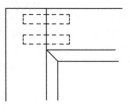

- For a more decorative finish you could work a molding instead of the simple chamfer or rounding. If you intend to fit a raised panel, you should choose a molding section to match any decoration on the raised panel. At a corner you can miter the molding and use tenons or dowels in the same way as that described for the chamfer.

- There is another way if you have a cutter with the reverse pattern of the molding. You can use this to cut across rail ends to match, so the assembled meeting parts close together and look like a well-cut miter in the corner.

- Not every door can be made with a single panel. You can divide into any number of panels and decorate round their edge framing in any of the ways described for outside framing. Deal with intermediate pieces as though they were two-sided corner joints. Groove both sides of the meeting part and cut back each tenon to both groove depths. Miter any meeting moldings.

- For some doors, you might find it satisfactory to leave a plywood panel without added decoration, particularly if it is to serve a utilitarian purpose or is to have a painted finish. Attractively veneered plywood will have sufficient decoration in itself.

- If you want to add decoration to a plywood-paneled door, put moldings on the surface. These can be bought strip moldings, or you can make them with your router. If you have a radius attachment for your router, you can make curved moldings for concave or convex corners in the decoration.

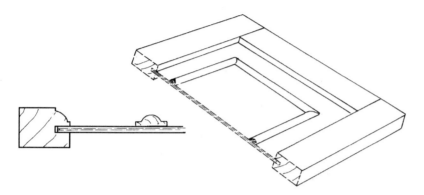
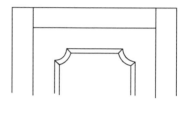

- Make a plywood panel look like a raised wood panel by gluing on a center piece. It can be another piece of plywood, but its edges will not look right unless all the panel is painted. If you glue on a thin piece of solid wood, its edges can be decorated by beveling or just chamfering, possibly to complement the edge decoration on the door.

- For good-quality furniture or built-in cabinets, you will almost certainly want to fit the doors with solid-wood raised or fielded panels. There are many cutters available to produce a variety of fielded edges or recesses around the panel. Your choice might depend on what you have and the power of your router, but you should also consider the purpose of the door—modern or reproduction, utility or part of some well-decorated furniture.

- In the days before portable electric routers when raising a panel had to be done with planes, the basic edge section was usually quite simple. A problem with this section is the way the tapered edge fits into a parallel groove. With expansion and contraction of the wood in its width, the tightness of fit will vary. If you are making reproduction furniture or want to produce only a simple fielded edge, you can get a router cutter to make a very similar section but with a parallel part to fit the groove and avoid variations in fit. (See top of page 86.)

- Not all traditional raised panels were made with these plain bevels, but those with an elaborate curved cross section would have required considerable skill with special planes and are less common. However, if you are reproducing furniture of a particular region, you should check whether a special form is usual. These and other modern sections are fairly easy to produce with a router, but you should always remember that the panel does not stand alone. It will be surrounded by framing that might be decorated, and other parts in the vicinity could also carry decoration. You can overdo decoration and spoil the effect. Relate the raised-panel decoration to that of nearby decorated parts. Some of the panel sections for which you can get cutters follow traditional and new forms.

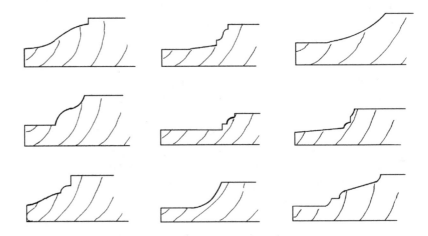

- With a router, you can make moldings on curved as well as straight edges, so you can shape the inner edges of door framing, and if there is a raised panel, it can be shaped to match. For some furniture, you can curve all inner framing edges, but with most doors you will probably find it advisable to confine shaping to the inner edge of the top of the doorframe. For the sake of appearance, leave enough solid wood across the top to be about the same width as the sides. Too much will look cumbersome, and too little will appear fragile. Balance the visual effect with a wider piece across the bottom of the door.

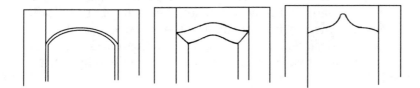

CHAPTER 19

Room divider

A ROOM DIVIDER or a two-sided bookcase can be made of veneered particleboard, which has many advantages for such a project. It comes in many widths and keeps its shape without warping or twisting, but it is unsuitable for edge shaping or molding, so designs have to be plain and angular. Glued dado joints can be cut with a router, and those are the only joints needed for this project.

Particleboard should be obtained veneered on its faces and edges. Also, have enough strip veneer to cover cut ends. A thickness of ¾ inch is suitable if you are working close to the suggested sizes. There are two upright divisions. They are important to brace the assembly and keep it in shape. If you do not want them where shown, others can be arranged toward the sides of shelves or elsewhere, but include sufficient edgewise parts to give stiffness.

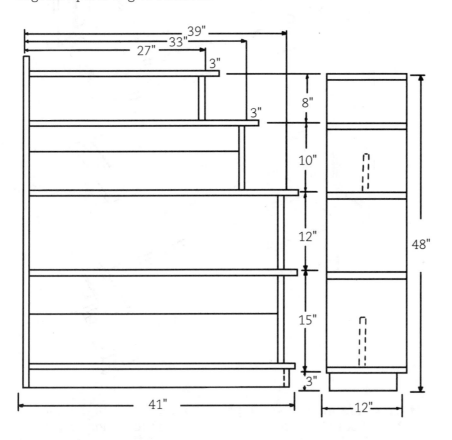

- Mark out the backboard first; this will give you the shelf spacing for other parts. (See top of page 90.)

- Cut the shelves to extend 3 inches past the uprights. Veneer the projecting ends of the parts cut so far.

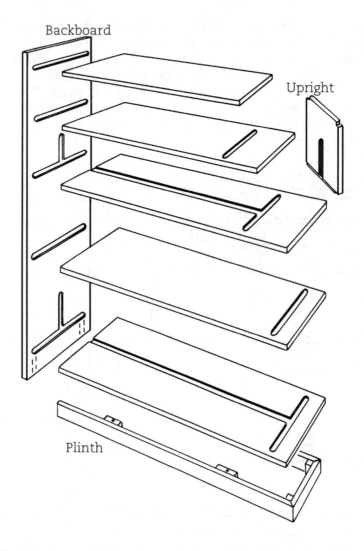

Backboard

Upright

Plinth

- The joints are dadoes, stopped about ¾ inch from the sides and about ¼ inch deep. You can square the corners with a chisel or leave them rounded. If the dadoes are cut with two or more passes of a smaller cutter, the ends can be nearly square with rounded corners. In any case, the other parts have to be shaped to fit. All dadoes in this project will have the same sections, so prepare your equipment for a run of similar cuts.

- Cut all the joints for the shelves to the backboard.

- Mark and cut the dadoes in the shelves for the short uprights.

- Check the shelf spacings on the backboard plus the depth of the shelf dadoes for the height of the shelf uprights. Cut all these joints.

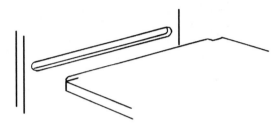

- It may be sufficient to fit the two upright divisions into dadoes only at their ends but you can cut shallow dadoes in the shelves as well if you think they would improve construction.

- The plinth is set back ¾ inch under the bottom shelf. Make its parts. At the outer corners, cut miters, which can be strengthened with wood blocks glued inside. At the backboard end, it should be sufficient to screw through from the back. Along the plinth sides, screw on wood blocks both ways when you join the plinth to the bottom shelf.

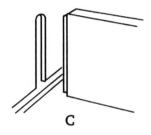

C

- Assemble all parts in one gluing operation, but the short uprights and the long vertical pieces will have to be joined to the shelves before they are joined to the backboard. You can use screws through the backboard into the joints if the rear surface will be hidden against a wall. You can also drive screws upward through shelves into the short uprights because the screw heads will be below eye level and usually not noticed. Small plastic connectors sold for particleboard assembly may be used if you think reinforcement of any joints is necessary, but tightly glued dado joints should have ample strength.

- Some plastic veneer will not require finishing, but otherwise polish in the same way as for solid wood.

Materials list   (All ¾-inch veneered particleboard)

1 backboard	12 × 51
3 shelves	12 × 42
1 shelf	12 × 36
1 shelf	12 × 30
1 upright	12 × 15
1 upright	12 × 12
1 upright	12 × 10
1 upright	12 × 8
1 upright	8 × 39
1 upright	6 × 33
2 plinths	3 × 41
1 plinth	3 × 12

Router carving

ALTHOUGH A ROUTER cannot be used for the sort of relief or three-dimensional carving that is possible with chisels and gouges, there are several ways to decorate your work with router cuts or to use the router for part of the work that will be completed with hand tools.

The simplest form of decoration is with incised grooves. Examples are shown in chapters 3 and 6. The effectiveness of this work is due to the play of light across the cuts, which need not be deep but should have clean, sharp edges. You can make V-shaped or rounded cuts, and in some places flat-bottomed grooves are effective. Having a groove depth equal to its width should be satisfactory.

- Drawer fronts are good places for incised decoration. Use guides for straight lines and those that are parts of circles, otherwise deviations will be obvious and spoil appearance. It may be sufficient just to work borders. With a stack of drawers of different depths, this should look good. Corners of the borders can be square or patterned.

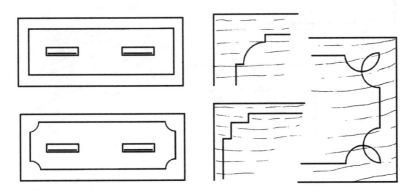

- You can include diagonal lines, but consider the overall appearance of the piece. This will have main outlines that are horizontal and vertical. Arranging diagonal lines that are too large or prominent can spoil the effect. Restrained diagonal lines are acceptable. With two drawer handles you can have some lines cross between them. With a central knob, the lines can be taken toward it.

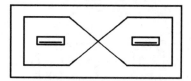 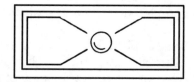

- On a drawer front or other expanse of wood of sufficient width, make a border, then further lines incised inside it. This is usually best with a straight border and any pattern arranged on the lines inside it. You can incise the outer lines with a square bottom and the inner lines **V**- or round-bottomed.

- A further step is to inlay border strips using wood of a contrasting color. This might be sufficient decoration, or you can work an incised pattern inside. You can make the border with stopped mitered corners, but it is easier and just as attractive to take cuts to the edges. You can achieve accuracy by first cutting the grooves one way only and gluing the strips in them, then cutting the grooves the other way across them.

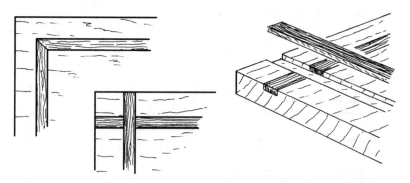

- Besides geometric and formal line patterns, you can cut outlines of flowers, birds, animals, and other natural things. You can decorate children's furniture with animals and cartoon characters. Do not attempt too much detail. Avoid angular shapes or very small patterns; the router will round some corners that should be sharp. For a bold treatment, this does not matter, but otherwise you might have to do some work with a knife or chisel.

- You can cut away a level background with more precision with a router than hand carving tools. This can be done as a preliminary to hand carving, although raising a flat outline in relief may be all you want, as with letters for a name board or a single motif.

- To start sinking a background, first go around the outline to the depth you want with a **V** or rounded cutter. If you want the design to stand out, undercut with a dovetail cutter. The wood for undercutting should be an even-grained nonbrittle hardwood to reduce the risk of breaking 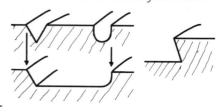 out. It helps to have a border enclosing the design to provide a bearing for the base of the router. Remove the waste between the outlining cuts with an end cutter set to the depth you want. A fairly shallow background cut should be enough for the design to stand out.

- You can work a single motif on a bookend in this way or cut a series of letters or numbers, all within borders. Leave the background as it comes from the tool, or go over it with a patterned punch. You might paint the background and varnish the raised parts, but the differences in texture will probably provide enough contrast to emphasize the shape.

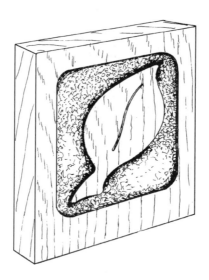

Welsh dresser

A UNIT WITH A broad working top over drawers and cupboard space has uses in almost any room in the home. With shelves above it, it becomes what was traditionally known as a Welsh dresser, for use in the kitchen or dining room. If made of a good-quality hardwood, with or without the shelves, the unit makes an attractive piece for living room or bedroom. If made of softwood and painted, it provides plenty of storage space in a den, workshop, or laundry room. The shelves are not a structural part of the lower unit, so they can be added later or can be removed to alter the use of the dresser.

The sizes suggested will produce a unit of useful size. If you alter the size, do not make the doors much wider than they are high. The number of drawers may be reduced to two.

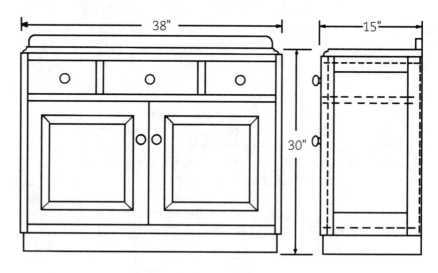

Most of the parts are drawn 1 inch thick. There are tenoned joints to cut and plywood panels to let in. The grooves for tenons may be ⅜ inch or ½ inch wide. The plywood might be the same, although ¼-inch plywood or even ⅛-inch hardboard would be adequate for a painted finish. You may alter the wood thickness to suit the grooves and tenons most conveniently made with your cutters. Thicknesses could go up to 1⅛ inches or down to ⅞ inch, but do not use wood less than ¾ inch thick.

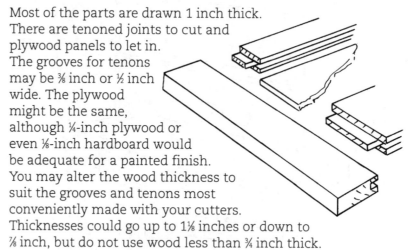

The main parts are a pair of end frames, three horizontal frames, and a top. They may be made independently and joined after they have been assembled.

- Start with the pair of ends. Groove the strips to take the plywood panels. Cut tenons on the short pieces, either the same thickness as the plywood or thicker, with the grooves enlarged at the ends of the sides to suit. Rabbet the rear edges to take the plywood back. (See margin illustration.)

- Assemble the ends. Glue drawer guides across inside the panels, level with the adjoining surfaces. There is no need to make cut joints for these guides.

- The three horizontal frames fit level with the sides at the front and against the plywood back. Their ends fit between the framed ends. All three frames are the same size, but they differ in detail. Only the fronts are normally visible, so they can be the same wood as the ends, with a cheaper wood for the inside parts.

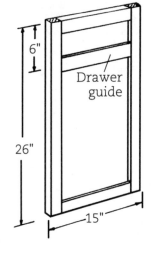

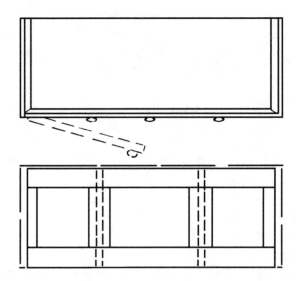

- At the top, the frame will be covered by a solid wood piece. It has two drawer guides as well as the end pieces to tenon to back and front. The frame below the drawers is the same, but you should close it with plywood. Groove the parts to take three pieces of plywood. (See top of page 100.)

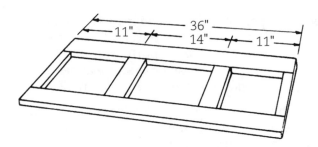

- At the bottom, most of the width is taken up by a piece of ½-inch plywood, but it fits in a rabbet, so its front edge is hidden. There is no need to put strips in the drawer-guide positions unless you think your plywood needs stiffening.

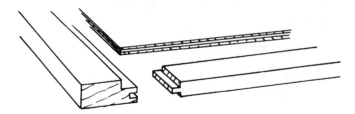

- Make two drawer divisions from solid wood, with the grain of the main part lengthwise but the grain of the front upright. Tongue-and-groove the parts together and drill for three dowels upward and downward. (See margin illustration.)

- Mark and drill for ½-inch dowels between the frames and ends. For additional strength, drill for screws through the narrow end pieces.

- Have the back plywood ready to overlap top and bottom frames and fit into the end rabbets.

- Join the parts made so far and temporarily screw in the back to hold the assembly square. You will probably want to remove it for access when fitting the drawers.

- Make and fit the plinth as described for the chest of drawers (chapter 17).

- The doors fit inside their framing. Make them with raised panels (chapter 18). Fit hinges and spring or magnetic catches. If the catches do not also act as stops, put in short pieces of wood for the doors to close against at top and bottom.

- Make and fit the drawers before adding the top, so you can see inside to check on them. Although they could be stopped by hitting the plywood back when they are pushed in, it will be better to make them slightly shorter and fit stops.

- Make the drawer fronts to fit in their openings. You can make small beads along their top and bottom edges. Make the sides the same depth. Cut grooves for the bottom in all these pieces. There are several ways to join the sides to the fronts, but the best joints are dovetails, with the bottom grooves hidden by *half tails*. The back may also be dovetailed or let into dadoes. Try the fits of the drawers before sliding their bottoms in.

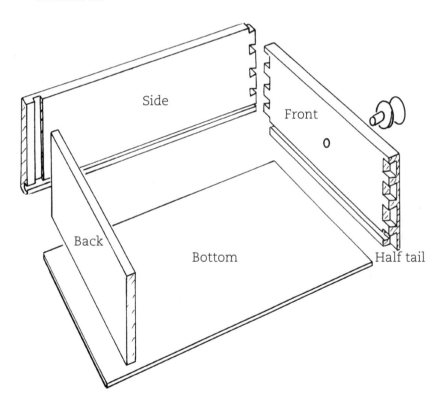

Side

Front

Back

Bottom

Half tail

- Any type of handles may be used for the doors and drawers, but to follow tradition, they should be turned knobs with dowel backs.

- Make the solid-wood top to overlap the plywood back and go to within about ⅜ inch of the counter surfaces at ends and front. Leave the rear edge square, but round or mold the other edges. Join the top to its frame with glue and screws driven upward.

- If the unit is to be used without the upper shelves, you can fit a strip along the rear edge to prevent articles falling over the back or marking a wall. Round the ends and use dowels into the top. If you may want to add the shelves later, attach the strip without glue so it can be removed.

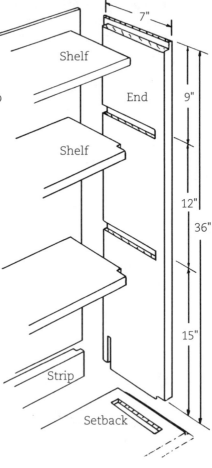

- The shelves are made like a bookcase, with a plywood back and an overhanging molded top. Arrange the overall width to be set back a short distance from the molded edges of the top of the lower unit.

- Make the pair of shelf ends. Rabbet the rear edges for the back.

- Make the shelves with stopped dado joints. The top shelf fits in a rabbet and will be hidden, so it need not be stopped.

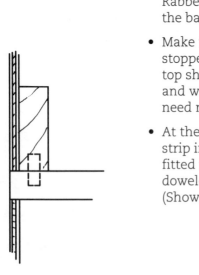

- At the bottom, notch a strip into the ends to be fitted inside the back and doweled downward. (Shown at left.)

- All the forward edges may be beaded.

- Assemble the parts and cut the dadoes in the top of the lower unit, but do not join it yet.

- The top of the shelf unit may be decorated with applied molding across the front and ends. Some Victorian Welsh dressers had large and complicated moldings, but modern design is usually more modest. This is an opportunity to use your molding bits to make a design using several pieces of wood mitered at the corners; one arrangement is shown. Allow for a strip overhanging and fit other molded pieces below it.

- Stain and polish or finish with paint to suit the wood and surroundings.

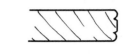

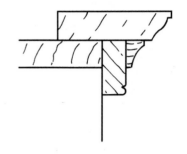

Materials list

4 end frames	1 × 2 × 27
4 end frames	1 × 2 × 15
2 end strips	⅜ × 3 × 15
2 end panels	13 × 24 × ¼ (plywood)
5 horizontal frames	1 × 3 × 37
1 horizontal frame	1½ × 3 × 37
6 horizontal frames	1 × 1½ × 14
4 horizontal frames	1 × 3 × 14
1 bottom	14 × 37 × ½ (plywood)
2 dividers	10 × 14 × ¼ (plywood)
1 divider	12 × 14 × ¼ (plywood)
2 divisions	1 × 5 × 15
2 divisions	1 × 2 × 6
8 door strips	1 × 2 × 20
2 door panels	¾ × 16 × 17
1 plinth	1 × 3 × 38
2 plinths	1 × 3 × 15
1 back	27 × 38 × ¼ (plywood)
2 drawer fronts	1 × 5 × 12
1 drawer front	1 × 5 × 15
6 drawer sides	⅝ × 5 × 15
2 drawer backs	⅝ × 5 × 12
1 drawer back	⅝ × 5 × 15
2 drawer bottoms	12 × 15 × ¼ (plywood)
1 drawer bottom	15 × 15 × ¼ (plywood)

1 unit top	1 × 15 × 39
1 top strip	1 × 2 × 38
2 shelf sides	1 × 7 × 38
3 shelves	1 × 7 × 36
1 bottom strip	1 × 3 × 36
1 back	36 × 36 × ¼ (plywood)

Top molding to suit your router bits

Table lamp stand

MULTIPLE BEADS or *flutes* can be very effective for a lamp stand and can be cut with several passes of a single bit. However, multiple bits will form a group of three or more at one time, ensuring accuracy and speeding the work.

Besides cuts on flat surfaces, you can use a router on round work. If you have a lathe that can be locked at a set number of positions in a circumference, you may be able to mount a router to make a bead or flute lengthwise, then move the wood to the next position and do it again until the circuit is complete.

The patterns go back in history. There are Greek and Persian stone pillars with lengthwise decoration of this sort. Pictures of these pillars may give you ideas for patterns to work with your router.

Making multiple cuts means that wood has to be cut exactly to size, with considerable care in setting and using the router cutters. Combinations of turning and router cuts are outside the scope of this book, but there are many pillarlike parts that you can make with flat surfaces.

Table and stool legs are possibilities. They require four parts being made to match, which may be difficult until you have had some practice. A single column is a better choice, and the example suggested is a table lampstand.

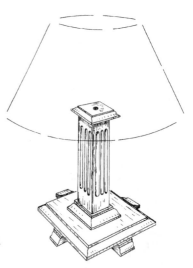

The column is made of two pieces joined. You can cut grooves, either square section or round, for the electric wires to pass through. If the woods match and the joint line comes in a hollow in the pattern, the division will not be very apparent. (See top left of page 106.)

You have a choice of many patterns, which may be full-length or stopped. If you decide to cut right through, start with the wood too long; then any inaccuracies at the start and finish of a cut will be removed. (See top right of page 106.)

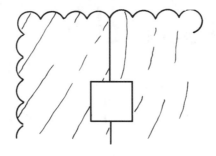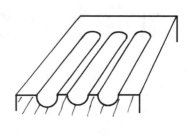

Each side may be completely covered, or you may leave flat wood outside and between cuts. If you decide to bead all over, the width must be planned to suit an exact number of cuts. A hollow at the center will hide a join.

Flutes or reeds may meet, but it is probably wiser to leave flat surfaces between or round the tops where they adjoin. Angular cuts are possible. Much of the attraction of lengthwise cuts is the way light and shade affect them. Deep **V** cuts cast good shadows.

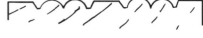
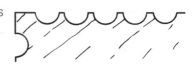

If you arrange flat surfaces between cuts, it is easier to make a pattern symmetrical. Work from opposite edges, and the central division will look satisfactory, even if its width is not quite what you originally intended. Interesting results can be achieved by using a cutter intended for making a molding on an edge but letting it cut on both sides of a hollow. Experiment with your bits on

scrapwood to see what patterns can be built up. Try the cuts taken the full length and stopped all on a line drawn squarely across. If there will be pieces larger than the pillar at each end, as in this lampstand, cutting right through can be effective, but stopped cuts have a neat appearance.

The lamp stand should be made of an attractive hardwood, but choose wood that will cut cleanly to reduce the hand work and sanding needed to get a satisfactory finish. Suggested sizes are given, but sizes may vary considerably, and you may want to alter sections to suit your cutters.

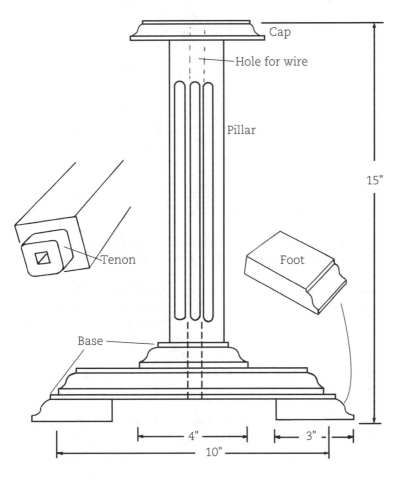

- Prepare the wood for the pillar. Groove centrally on two pieces of 1-x-2-inch section, then glue them together. Start with the wood a few inches too long.

- Mark to length, allowing for the bottom to have a tenon through the first part of the base. The top is made the same way, but tenoned only halfway through the cap.

- Mark out and cut your pattern on all four faces. If one or both ends of the pattern is to be stopped, pencil squarely around all four faces.

- The cap is 5 inches square. Cut it to size with carefully squared edges.

- Prepare squares in a similar way for the base.

- Drill through the centers of all three pieces, large enough to pass the electric wires.

- Mark the tenon on the bottom of the pillar, a mortise on the base. Round the corners of the tenon to fit the mortise or leave the tenon with square corners and trim the mortise square with a chisel.

- At the top, make a mortise in the cap only halfway through, with a tenon on the pillar to suit.

- Mold all four edges of each flat square piece—a simple rounding, reeds, or any molding for which you have a cutter.

- Make four feet, 2 inches wide and 3 inches long. It may be easier to cut the molded ends if you start with wider wood or clamp all four pieces together so the router cutter can pass over all ends in one cut.

- Glue the parts together. You can also place screws upward through the base pieces.

- Finish with stain and polish; then add the electrical fittings.

Materials list

2 pillars	1 × 2 × 14
1 cap	¾ × 5 × 6
1 base	1 × 4 × 5
1 base	1 × 10 × 11
4 feet	1 × 2 × 4

Plywood magazine trough

A HANDLED CARRIER for magazines and newspapers can be used beside a chair or taken wherever needed. This project is a two-compartment trough made entirely of plywood. It may be given a clear finish, but although well-cut plywood edges may be attractive, most users will prefer a painted finish. It may be decorated with decals or incised patterns on the side panels.

This magazine rack or trough is introduced here as the type of construction suitable for quantity production. If you make *templates* for the parts and use the router bits along a guide, you can undertake a modest production run and make magazine troughs at an economical cost. The following instructions are for making one magazine trough, but for a quantity using templates, the same steps should be done to every piece before moving on.

The sizes shown are for a roomy rack, but they are easily reduced. Gather your usual magazines and measure them. It is always better to have too much capacity than not enough. Any type of plywood may be used. Douglas fir should respond to sharp cutters, but good edges and grooves may be easier to cut in plywood made from closer-grained, harder woods. (See top of page 110.)

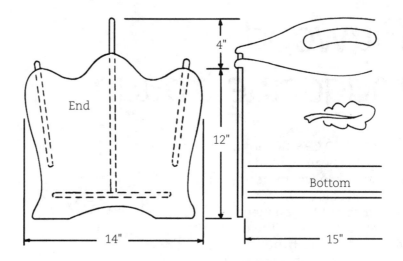

End

4"

12"

14"

Bottom

15"

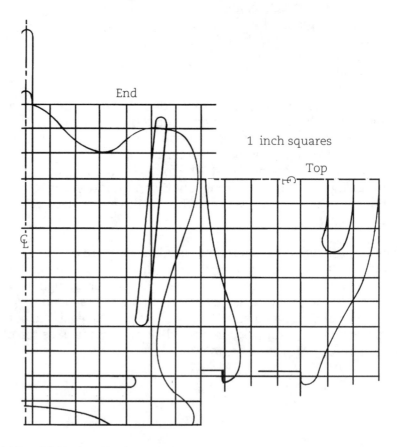

End

1 inch squares

Top

CL

- Start with the two ends. Use the squared drawing to obtain the outline and the location of grooves. (See bottom illustration on page 110.)

- To reduce the risk of breaking out at the corners, cut the dado grooves before cutting the outline. The grooves should be a tight fit on the plywood and taken halfway through the thickness.

- Cut the outlines. Sand if necessary to take sharpness off the edges.

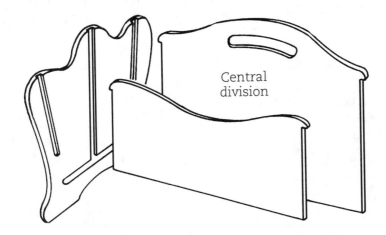

Central division

- Mark out the central division. Use the squared drawing as a guide to shaping the top. Cut to shape with all edges square, then round the hand hole and the shaped top. Curve over the parts that cover the grooves in the ends.

- Mark and cut the two outer panels in a similar way. The squared drawing shows the shape of the hollowed top edge, which should be rounded in cross section.

- The bottom is a parallel piece the same length as the upright parts of the other pieces. Round its outer edges and the bottom edges of the side panels to match the curves left by the router bits at the ends of the grooves.

- If you are using incised decoration on the side panels, do it before assembly. You can cut shallow relief carving. A name can be cut with rounded hollows. Or a simple decoration such as a leaf can be cut as lines with a fine curved or pointed bit—freehand for one-off but using a template if you are making several troughs.

- Join the parts with glue and fine nails or pins driven from outside the ends. You may drive a few fine screws upward through the bottom into the central division. Set nail heads below the surface and cover them with wood filler.

- Finish the wood with several coats of paint. An incised design might be picked out in another color. If you put decals on the paint, cover them with clear varnish.

Materials list

(All ½-inch plywood)

2 ends	13 × 14
1 division	14 × 18
2 side panels	9 × 18
1 bottom	10 × 18

Revolving holdall

A REVOLVING HOLDALL is similar to some bookcases and display stands where you can turn the unit around so that any of the four sides faces you. There are two compartments able to take books of the size of this one, a cupboard with a door, and a block of drawers.

The arrangement may be altered, depending on your requirements. There might be four book compartments, or if you have a hobby with many small items to store, you may want drawers all around. The arrangement and sizes may be varied, but the four sections must be the same size. (See page 114.)

The unit is supported on crossed strips that form feet. On this goes a lazy-Susan bearing, which comes as a unit to screw on. The larger type, often used for revolving seats in boats, will be suitable; any size from 6 inches to 10 inches will do.

If the holdall is for use in a shop or hobby room, it need not have molded edges, and many parts may be of plywood with edge grain exposed. For a more important situation, use a good furniture hardwood. Some parts, particularly the top and bottom, can be made of veneered particleboard or plywood with solid wood edging. The pieces that make up the compartments should be solid wood with vertical grain.

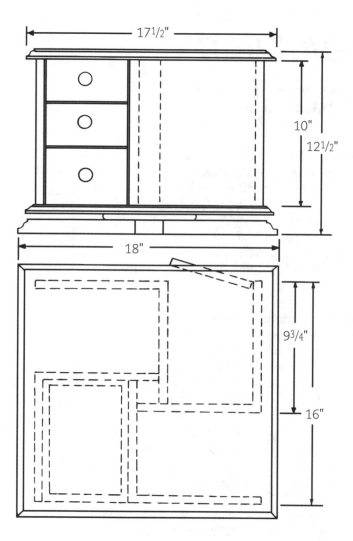

- Set out the center post and four divisions full size. Make the outer pieces. These parts are the same, whatever storage arrangements you choose. Cut tongue-and-groove joints at the outer corners. At the center, the divisions may be drilled for a few screws into the post. (See top of page 115.)

- At the top edges of the outer pieces, place square strips for screwing to the top. Set the ends of the strips back far enough to hide them and clear a door or drawer front. At the bottom, screws will be driven upward.

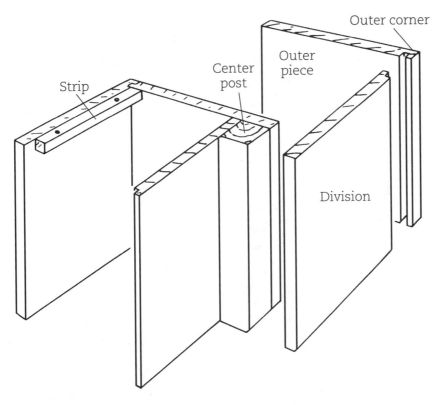

Strip

Center post

Outer piece

Outer corner

Division

- The top and bottom are identical, 18 inches square. They may be solid wood. If you use veneered plywood or particleboard, make a 2-inch wide solid-wood edging, preferably with a tongue-and-groove joint and mitered corners. Mold the edges with any design you wish. (Shown at right.)

- Make the drawer fronts any height to suit your needs, but they look best if the deepest one is lowest. At the top, the drawer sides will come below the square screw strip, but the drawer front projects up to overlap its end. The front also overlaps the drawer bottom, but the sides are above it. For these small drawers, it will be satisfactory for the sides to be glued into rabbets and strengthened with a few pins. The back is held with tongue and groove joints, and the bottom is nailed from below. (See top of page 116.)

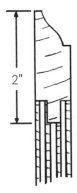

2"

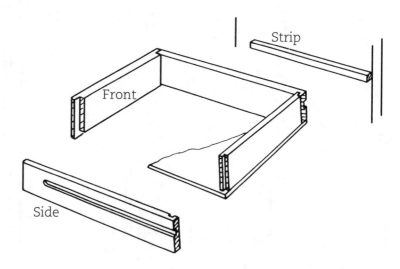

- Make the drawers an easy fit between the compartment sides. Groove the drawer sides to slide on ¼-x-½-inch strips. Fit knobs or handles to the drawer fronts. Defer final assembly until the drawers can be tried in place.

- If there is to be a door to a compartment, it may be a plain piece of wood hinged at one side and closing against the screw strip with a spring or magnetic catch. Fit a handle to match those of the drawers.

- Assemble the vertical parts. Mark their outline on the underside of the top and the upper surface of the bottom. Drill the bottom for screws.

- Invert the parts on the top, with the marked position as a guide, and fit them with glue and screws through the strips.

- Put the bottom in place; glue and screw it on. Be careful to get parts parallel and square, particularly for drawers.

- Make the feet, halved together and with ends molded to match the other parts. (See next page.)

- Fit the lazy-Susan bearing according to the instructions supplied with it. Most have wood screws upward into the center of the unit bottom. The feet are then attached with a self-tapping screw in a counterbored hole up through each side of the feet.

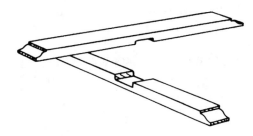

- After a trial assembly, remove the feet and finish the wood with stain and polish or to suit the situation. You can glue cloth under the ends of the feet.

Materials list

1 pillar	1½ × 1½ × 11
4 divisions	⅝ × 9 × 11
4 outer pieces	⅝ × 9½ × 11
4 screw strips	⅝ × ⅝ × 9
1 top	⅝ × 18 × 18
1 bottom	⅝ × 18 × 18
2 feet	1 × 2 × 19
1 door	⅝ × 7 × 11

Drawer fronts ⅝ and sides ½ as required

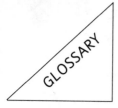
GLOSSARY

Many special terms are used in woodworking. Those that follow are particularly applicable to the use of routers.

allen key Hexagonal rod used to fit socket in screw head for turning it.

arris Sharp angle between two surfaces.

back flap Hinge with long arm for table drop leaf.

bead Convex rounded molding.

bearing Ball-bearing guide at end of cutter.

bit The cutter driven by a router.

bottom-cut A bit for plunging, cutting on its end and circumference.

cavetto Molding with concave cut.

collet Round socket into which a bit is fitted.

core box cutter Tool for cutting semicircular grooves.

cove Concave molding.

cutter Part of a bit that cuts, or the whole bit.

dado A groove, as for taking the end of a shelf.

deckle edge Wavy edge.

diamond whetstone Tool for honing TCT cutters.

face molding Molding on a broad surface instead of an edge.

fielded panel Door panel with raised center.

fence A guide to control the distance of a cut from an edge.

fillet Narrow strip, as for holding a mirror in a rabbet.

flute   Lengthwise groove in cutter.

HSS   High-speed steel.

jig   A device to provide control when cutting.

molding   Decoration in length, usually on an edge.

mortise-and-tenon joint   A rectangular tenon on an end fits a matching mortise hole. When cut with a router, corners may be rounded.

no-load speed   Revolutions per minute when the router is not cutting.

ogee   Molded edge with concave and convex curves in section.

ovolo   Molded edge with a bead section.

pin guide   Extension at end of cutter to control depth of cut.

plunge router   Tool in which the bit can be lowered into the wood.

profile   Outline, external or internal.

rabbet   Angular recess, as in a picture frame.

raised panel   Door panel with projecting center.

reed   Long narrow groove.

scribe   Reverse cut to fit on a molding section.

sinking   Cutting a lowered background in a carving.

spindle molder   A tool using cutters similar to those of a router but in which the wood is moved against a revolving cutter.

stopped dado (or other joint)   Not cut right through.

sub base Additional router base for special work.

TCT Tungsten-carbide tipped.

template, templet A shaped guide for a cut.

tongue and groove Joint with a projection on one piece fitting into the other pieces.

tracking Maintaining a straight cut.

*Boldface numbers refer to art

Other Bestsellers of
Related Interest

**THE COMPLETE BOOK OF HOME INSPECTION
—2nd Edition—Norman Becker, P.E.**
Evaluate a property inside and out. To find problems
when inspecting a new home or when maintaining your
present home, consult this valuable guide for advice
that's guaranteed to take the guesswork and stress out of
home inspection for the buyer *and* the owner. Now
updated to cover current building materials, construction techniques, and home heating, electrical, and
plumbing systems, it walks you through every square
inch of a house and shows you how to determine its
soundness. 288 pages, 155 illustrations. Book No. 4100,
$12.95 paperback only

**ALL THUMBS GUIDE TO HOME ENERGY SAVINGS
—Robert W. Wood**
Slash your energy consumption in half with only a few of
the simple, inexpensive home improvements discussed
in this hey-I-really-can-do-this book. You'll discover how
to seal doors and windows; insulate attics, basements,
and crawl spaces; insulate water heaters and pipes; stop
faucet and toilet leaks; install energy-efficient lighting,
attic fans, and roof turbines; use central heating and
cooling more efficiently; and much more. 144 pages, at
least 150 illustrations—two-color throughout. Book No.
4244, $9.95 paperback only

ALL THUMBS GUIDE TO PAINTING, WALLPAPERING, AND STENCILING—Robert W. Wood

Make your home look beautiful with a fresh coat of paint or new wallpaper. Wood shows you how to add a decorative touch to any or all rooms in the house. You'll learn how to patch holes in drywall, choose the right paint or wallpaper, apply the paper and clean up, use stencils for dramatic effect, and choose and use the tools of the trade. This helpful guide gives you easy-to-follow, step-by-step instructions, clear, how-to line drawings *for each step* . . . a convenient lay-flat binding . . . detachable tip cards with safety precautions, troubleshooting steps, and shopping lists . . . and an all-inclusive glossary of terms. 144 pages, 180 illustrations. Book No. 4060, $9.95 paperback only

HOME PLUMBING ILLUSTRATED—R. Dodge Woodson

Save money, time, and frustration by doing your own home plumbing. This book gives you the confidence to tackle any residential plumbing job imaginable. From the basics to advanced plumbing techniques, it covers tools and materials; reading blueprints and designs; plumbing layouts and material takeoffs; cost estimating and material acquisitions; underground plumbing; the drain waste-and-vent system (DWV); installing fixtures, water pumps, and conditioners; and passing an inspection. 288 pages, 200 illustrations. Book No. 4163, $14.95 paperback only

FENCES, DECKS, AND OTHER BACKYARD PROJECTS —3rd Edition—Dan Ramsey

Transform your backyard living space from the ordinary into the extraordinary with this fantastic idea book. Packed with step-by-step instructions and hundreds of illustrations, this updated guide shows you how to choose, design, prepare, build, and maintain all types of beautiful fences, decks, and other outdoor structures. Veteran how-to author Dan Ramsey offers a veritable bonanza of backyard building ideas. 288 pages, over 300 illustrations. Book No. 4071, $14.95 paperback, $24.95 hardcover

PLAYHOUSES, GAZEBOS, AND SHEDS
—Percy W. Blandford

Build a workshop or playhouse in your backyard—and save hundreds of dollars by doing it yourself! All you need is a few basic tools and materials and *Playhouses, Gazebos and Sheds!* Detailed instructions, step-by-step instructions, complete materials lists, and expert tips make this a onestop guide, no matter what your skill level. Blandford's clear and conversational writing style will guide you through even the largest of outdoor building projects with ease. 150 pages, 200 illustrations. Book No. 4077, $9.95 paperback only

Prices Subject to Change Without Notice.

Look for These and Other TAB Books at Your Local Bookstore

To Order Call Toll Free 1-800-822-8158
(24-hour telephone service available.)

or write to TAB Books, Blue Ridge Summit, PA 17294-0840.

Title	Product No.	Quantity	Price

☐ Check or money order made payable to TAB Books

Charge my ☐ VISA ☐ MasterCard ☐ American Express

Acct. No. _____ Exp. _____

Signature: _____

Name: _____

Address: _____

City: _____

State: _____ Zip: _____

Subtotal $ _____

Postage and Handling
($3.00 in U.S., $5.00 outside U.S.) $ _____

Add applicable state and local
sales tax $ _____

TOTAL $ _____

TAB Books catalog free with purchase; otherwise send $1.00 in check or money order and receive $1.00 credit on your next purchase.

Orders outside U.S. must pay with international money in U.S. dollars drawn on a U.S. bank.

TAB Guarantee: If for any reason you are not satisfied with the book(s) you order, simply return it (them) within 15 days and receive a full refund.

BC

Percy W. Blandford has been an avid woodworker for more than 55 years and a full-time how-to writer for 40 years. During that time he has written more than 4,000 magazine articles and 100 books, including *Backyard Builder's Bonanza*, *A Home Full of Furniture*, *One-Weekend Country Furniture Projects*, and *101 One-Weekend Toy Projects*.

About the author